The Etiquettes
of Spiritual Wayfaring & the Journey to God

Sayyid Muhammad Jawad Vazirifard

Copyright © 2022 by Hadi Institute

All rights reserved. No part of this may be reproduced, distributed, or transmitted in any form or by any means. This includes photocopying, recording, or other electronic or mechanical methods, without prior written permission of the publisher, except in the case of brief quotations embodied in critical reviews, certain noncommercial uses permitted by copyright law and for Islamic teaching purposes. For permission requests, please email publications@hadinstitute.com.

First Edition, 2022
ISBN: 9781737613916

Illustrations by: Sakina Abideen

Published by: Hadi Institute
Dearborn, Michigan
www.hadinstitute.com

In the name of Allah, the All-Beneficent, the All-Merciful

حاسبوا انفسكم
قبل ان تحاسبوا

"TAKE ACCOUNT OF YOURSELVES BEFORE YOU ARE TAKEN ACCOUNT OF."

~Prophet Muhammad (s)

Mustadrak al-Wasa'il, V, 12, p. 153.

Table of Contents

INTRODUCTION
    Translator's Preface   16
    Elite of the Elite   21
    Message of Condolences   25
    About the Author   27

THE LETTER   30

THE COMMENTARY
    Our Teacher's Statement   34

PART 1 – FOUNDATIONS
    Etiquette 1: Obligations and Prohibitions   40
    Etiquette 2: Attending to a Teacher   58
    Etiquette 3: Being Balanced   68

PART 2 – FRATERNITY
    Etiquette 4: Where Do You Sit?   72
    Etiquette 5: Friends of the Path   80
    Etiquette 6: Ahl al-Dunya   86

PART 3 – FOCUS
    Etiquette 7: Concern Yourself with Yourself   94
    Etiquette 8: Make Silence Your Motto   120
    Etiquette 9: Avoid Your Desires   128

PART 4 – FREEDOM
    Etiquette 10: Deliberation and Consultation   136
    Etiquette 11: Mysteries of the Path   142
    Etiquette 12: A Positive Outlook   148
    Etiquette 13: Freeing the Soul   158
    Final Remarks   170

DISCLAIMER

This book has been written, translated, and annotated as a stand-alone work. However, the reader is still advised to consult an expert when appropriate. Ayatullah Muhammad Baqir Tahriri has said, "Studying Islamic narrations or books of Islamic ethics and wayfaring, without referring to a teacher and without a proficient understanding of the principles of this journey of self-refinement…can sometimes lead to ideological, spiritual, psychological, or physical abnormalities."[1]

---

1. True Servitude and the Reality of Knowledge, Muhammad Baqir Tahriri, p. 74-5.

Translator's Preface

يَا أَيُّهَا الْإِنسَانُ إِنَّكَ كَادِحٌ إِلَىٰ رَبِّكَ كَدْحًا فَمُلَاقِيهِ[2]

"O man! You are laboring toward your Lord laboriously, and you will encounter Him."

---

2. Holy Qur'an, 84:6

We are travelers journeying towards Allah (s)—
"Indeed to your Lord is the return"³—yet we remain
"disregardful in obliviousness."⁴ Those living in the epicenter
of heedlessness and negligence, the modern West, are
especially susceptible to losing their way. Many recognize
the spiritual dangers posed by the conditions we live in, but
few identify sources of guidance to satiate their spiritual
needs. This challenge is aggravated by the prevalence of
pseudo-spirituality, lacking any connection to the Divine.
With this challenge in mind, I humbly offer this translation
in hopes of gaining Allah's (s) satisfaction and pleasing the
Imam of the Age (a.f.).

The story of this book, titled ادب سیر in its original
Farsi, begins with the great mystic, philosopher, and
commentator of the Holy Qur'an, Allamah Sayyid
Muhammad Husayn Tabataba'i. Although best known for
his Tafsir al-Mizan, the heritage he bequeathed to those
wishing to travel the spiritual path is no less significant.
While many of Allamah's works have made their way into the
English corpus, we have yet to benefit from the treasures of
one of his students, Ayatullah Ali Pahlawani Tehrani, better
known as Ayatullah Sa'adat Parwar.

The Etiquettes consists of a letter written by Ayatullah
Sa'adat Parwar and a commentary on that letter authored

---

3. Holy Qur'an, 96:8 - إِنَّ إِلَىٰ رَبِّكَ ٱلرُّجْعَىٰ
4. Holy Qur'an, 21:1 - ٱقْتَرَبَ لِلنَّاسِ حِسَابُهُمْ وَهُمْ فِي غَفْلَةٍ مُعْرِضُونَ

by his student, Hujjatul Islam wal Muslimeen Dr. Sayyid Muhammad Jawad Vazirifard. A unique characteristic of this book is that it can assist a person at any stage of his or her spiritual journey, as it mostly includes practical advice on self-building.

However, some passages dive deeper into Islam's rich spiritual heritage and others are specific to those under the tutelage of a spiritual master. Such passages serve the dual purpose of assisting those with access to such a guide, and motivating those without such a guide to seek one. These were among the reasons why four of the esteemed students of Ayatullah Sa'adat Parwar, now teachers of *akhlaq* and practical *Irfan* in the Holy City of Qom, blessed this translation project.

Spiritual wayfaring is a process of continual self-purification to ascend to peaks of perfection and unite with Allah (s), but its methodology is extremely important. Thus, in order to assist the reader in understanding this text, I edited and annotated it by way of headings, subheadings, footnotes, and on rare occasions, adjustments to the original. In addition, I did not strictly adhere to a standard transliteration table for Arabic terminology in the hopes of simplifying the read. I extend my gratitude to all those sincere individuals who assisted me during the translation, editing, and publishing processes, while accepting full responsibility for all shortcomings.

I dedicate this effort, and any resulting reward, to my family. Words fail to appreciate my wife's patience, sacrifice, and support. I thank Allah (s) for blessing me with the best of travel companions. As for our parents, whatever good my wife and I perform is a result of their selfless love and prayers and we are forever grateful. In addition, our siblings' encouragement gave us the strength to begin and continue on this path. Finally, I am indebted to my children and the lessons they teach me daily. I pray that long after I am gone, they continue to act on these etiquettes.

I write this sitting between the graves of Allamah Tabataba'i and Ayatullah Sa'adat Parwar in the Holy Precinct of Sayyidah Fatimah Masumah (a). I ask Allah (s) that by the right of these pure souls, He grant us the sincerity necessary to benefit from these pages. Wassalaamu alaykum wa rahmatullah.

Abu'l Qasim
Qom al-Muqaddasah
Ramadhan 23, 1442 - May 6, 2021

Allamah Sayyid Ali Qadi & Allamah Tabataba'i

Elite of the Elite

"From among our chains of jurisprudence and divine wisdom within the *Hawza*…we have the elite of the elite who serve as role models for all, from the distinguished scholar to the youth. They are those who were not satisfied with just the apparent aspects of religion, but rather exerted great efforts and reached exalted stations on the path of gnosis, spiritual wayfaring, and *Tawhid*. Notably, this great movement of wayfaring did not come about by way of personal whims and fancies, rather they reached these exalted stations by way of the holy *shariah*.

This is the path of Sayyid Ali Qadi … His students were a source of blessing wherever they were. One example was Allamah Tabataba'i, who enlightened Qom with the light of the intellectual sciences… Do not define *Irfan* by way of words, phrases, and mental formulas as we do other subjects. Rather, *Irfan* is embodied in the likes of Sayyid Ali Qadi… While Allamah Tabataba'i was a philosopher and well-read in Theoretical *Irfan*, his legacy in *Irfan* is Practical *Irfan*, meaning wayfaring, instructions, and training wayfarers…[5]

Shaykh Ali [Sa'adat Parwar] embodied God-

---

5. Guzargah: Bayyanat-e-Maqam-e-Muazam-e-Rahbari darbare Ulama va Urafa, Husayn Khadimi, p. 21, 25, & 30; Payam Rahbar-e-Inqalab beh Kongereye Burzurgdasht Ayatullah Sayyid Ali Qadi, available at leader.ir.

consciousness and not being inclined to the lowly world in its real sense. He was from among the extraordinary people of our time whom we often fail to recognize… As the prophetic tradition states, 'Surely Allah (s) has hidden four things in four things.' One of the four things that Allah (s) has hidden is His choicest servants among the people. They sit and speak with the people like anyone else, but within these extraordinary souls exists an ocean [of *ma'arifah*]…"[6]

- Ayatullah Sayyid Ali Khamenei

---

6. Irfan-e-Amin, Muhammad Ali Tolaee, p. 262-5.

Ayatullah Ali Pahlawani Tehrani (Sa'adat Parwar)

Message of Condolences Offered on the Demise of Ayatullah Sa'adat Parwar

In the name of Allah, the Compassionate, the Merciful.

Respected Hujjatul Islam Aga Hajj Shaykh Hasan Pahlawani Tehrani,

It is with sadness and regret that we have received the news of the passing of your respected brother, the scholar who acted on his words, the mystic, the pious, the virtuous, the respected, Hajj Shaykh Ali Aga Pahlawani Tehrani [Sa'adat Parwar]. That great personality lived a pure life and with blessed efforts taught and propagated divine and monotheistic teachings. He was an example of sincerity. I pray that the pure and immaculate servant is enveloped by Divine grace, favor, mercy, and forgiveness, as is promised to Allah's (s) pious slaves. With heartfelt sincerity, I extend my condolences to you and the entire family of the deceased.

Wa salaamu alaykum wa rahmatullah

Sayyid Ali Khamenei

September 30, 2004[7]

---

7. Sulook-e-Sa'adat, Ali Ridha Saeedi, p. 15.

Ayatullah Ali Pahlawani Tehrani (Sa'adat Parwar)

About the Author of the Letter

Ayatullah Shaykh Ali Pahlawani Tehrani (Sa'adat Parwar) was born in the year 1926 to a religious family in Tehran, Iran. He completed his preliminary seminary education under the tutelage of Shaykh Muhammad Husayn Zahid and Shaykh Ali Akbar Burhan. In 1944, he moved to Qom where he reached the level of *Ijtihad*, studying Jurisprudence, the Principles of Jurisprudence, and Philosophy under Ayatullah Burujurdi, Imam Khomeini, and Allamah Tabataba'i. Beginning in 1951, he became one of the elite students of Allamah Tabataba'i in spiritual wayfaring and practical *Irfan*, attending to his teacher until Allamah's death in 1981. Thereafter, based on the instructions of his departed teacher, Ayatullah Sa'adat Parwar dedicated his life to training students in *akhlaq* and practical *Irfan* until his death in 2004. He is the author of many masterpieces, including Sirr al-Isra (Commentary on the Hadith of Miraj), Jilveh-ye-Noor (on the spiritual station of Sayyidah Fatimah Zahra (a)), Furoogh-e-Shahadat (An Esoteric Look at the Revolution of Imam Husayn (a)), al-Shumoos al-Mudheeah (Examining the coming of the Imam of the Era (a.f.)), and Jamal-e-Aftab (Commentary on the poetry of Hafiz in light of the Holy Qur'an and *Sunnah*). Today his students are among Qom's leading teachers of practical *Irfan* and are known for their God-consciousness, sincerity, and reliance upon the Holy Qur'an and Ahl ul-Bayt (a). Ayatullah Sa'adat Parwar is buried in Qom in the holy confines of the mausoleum of Sayyidah Fatimah Masuma (a).

Hujjatul Islam Dr. Sayyid Muhammad Jawad Vazirifard

About the Author of the Commentary

Hujjatul Islam wal Muslimeen Dr. Sayyid Muhammad Jawad Vazirifard was born in 1956 in the Holy City of Mashhad, Iran. After the completion of his preliminary studies, he moved to Tehran to pursue a degree in Mechanical Engineering and was active in the efforts that culminated in the victory of the Islamic Revolution in 1979. In 1983, Ustadh Vazirifard began his seminary studies at the Ferdowsi University in Mashhad, with a focus on Law and Islamic Legal Theory. He later obtained a Doctorate in Qur'anic & Hadith Sciences from Tarbiat Modares University in Tehran. In 1991, he became acquainted with the great gnostic *(arif)*, Ayatullah Sa'adat Parwar, and remained his devoted pupil until the Ayatullah's death in 2004. Ustadh Vazirifard has authored over a dozen books and is a recognized and respected teacher of ethics and practical *Irfan* in the Qom seminary. Ustadh Vazirifard is currently engaged in research, writing, teaching, and training students in spiritual wayfaring.

The Letter of Ayatullah Sa'adat Parwar

"*In the Name of the Most High:*

May I be ransomed for you! Considering my long-standing love for you and my friends wayfaring with me on this path, I found it necessary to mention some matters which are useful to the wayfarer (salik) on his journey to Allah. If these are acted upon, a hundred-year path is traversed in a single year.

1. *Perform the obligatory acts (wajibat) and avoid the prohibited ones (muharramat). After that, perform the recommended acts (mustahabat) to one's capacity and avoid the disliked acts (makruhat). From among the recommended acts, give a lot of importance to the Night Prayer (Salat al-Layl) and to wakefulness before the morning call to prayer (adhan). Also, one should not neglect performing the daily prayers at the beginning of their prescribed times, the recitation of the Holy Qur'an, and seeking the intercession of the Holy Prophet (s) and his family (a).*

2. *Attend to a spiritual teacher and act upon his statements. Relate all states (halat), stations (maqamat), visions (mushahadat), and even dreams encountered. Do not present your own view in relation to the teacher's view on spiritual wayfaring.*

3. *Avoid the extremes of excessiveness and deficiency in every matter.*

4. *Avoid listening to speech that distracts and divides one's attention. In addition, avoid sitting with those who are careless with their speech and actions, even if they are wayfarers.*

5. *Interacting with a self-vigilant wayfarer is very good. However, if he holds peculiar beliefs regarding the affairs of wayfaring, then only take into consideration that which your teacher instructs otherwise it will create*

divisiveness [and result in a wasted opportunity].

6. *Interacting with worldly people - those who only care about eating and sleeping, and going here-and-there - is harmful, except to the extent that is necessary.*

7. *The wayfarer must focus his attention on himself and attend to himself. He should not spend his life talking about this-or-that person, even if not backbiting them, and should avoid useless speech.*

8. *Make silence your motto, except when needed, because most slips are caused by the tongue.*

9. *Avoid selfish desires as much as possible and with discretion. In any matter in which [the nafs is overly inclined], perform an istikharah so that there is at least a justification for the act.*

10. *Do not get involved in any work or endeavor without deliberation, even if this takes a long time. In this regard, consulting with your spiritual teacher and fellow wayfarers is very necessary.*

11. *Do not share the spiritual matters that one encounters with anyone except for the spiritual teacher, until the wayfarer reaches the stage of certainty (itminan).*

12. *Avoid thinking negatively of Allah's servants. Instead, one should think of reforming one's self and becoming so introspective that the shortcomings of others become invisible to him. Note, however, that the obligation to enjoin good (al-amru bi al-ma'ruf) and forbid evil (al-nahyu an al-munkar) is another matter.*

13. *All of one's struggles and difficulties are to strengthen the spirit so the soul frees itself from this natural world. Efforts must be made to strengthen the spirit, which lies in giving importance to the matters mentioned in this letter as much as possible, and in avoiding the strengthening of one's material aspects more than is necessary."*

The Commentary of Ustadh Sayyid Muhammad Jawad Vazirifard

Our Teacher's Statement:

"May I be ransomed for you! Considering my long-standing love for you and my friends wayfaring with me on this path, I found it necessary to mention some matters which are useful to the wayfarer (salik) on his journey to Allah. If these are acted upon, a hundred-year path is traversed in a single year."

Love Between the Spiritual Teacher and His Student

When a spiritual teacher tells his student, "May I be ransomed for you," his words are not flattery. A spiritual teacher loves his student because the teacher's attention to the student results in the student gaining proximity to Allah (s). And that result is beloved to the teacher. A student may love his spiritual teacher, but he should not think it is one-sided. In fact, it is the spiritual teacher that brings about and instills love into the heart of the student.[8]

---

8. On the necessity of attending to a spiritual teacher, Ayatullah Sa'adat Parwar said, "Spiritual wayfaring and reaching the peaks of human perfection are more difficult than other matters and are not possible without a teacher and guide…one who himself was trained by a teacher…" Jamal-e-Aftab, Sa'adat Parwar, V. 3 p. 11.

Imam Ruhollah Khomeini stated, "Choose a teacher of morals for yourself, and arrange sessions for advice, counsel, and admonition. You cannot become refined by yourself…Why is it that the science of Jurisprudence (Fiqh) and the Principles of Jurisprudence (Usul al-Fiqh) require a teacher, and in fact every science and field requires a teacher or expert…However, in the fields of spiritual knowledge and ethics, which are the goals of the raising of the prophets and are among the most subtle and precise sciences, some say a teacher is not required?!" Combat with the Self, Sayyid Ruhollah Khomeini, p. 10.

Ayatuallah Tahriri quotes Allamah Qadi as having said, "If one spends half of his life in search of a complete spiritual teacher, he has not suffered loss." Ayatullah Tahriri then adds that one who acquires a teacher "should know that he has traversed a major portion of the journey and that this is a great blessing that Allah (s) has apportioned for him." Tahriri, p. 103-5.

Those still searching for uch a guide should not lose hope, as "Without a doubt, Allah (s), who is man's guide toward Himself, will help [a deserving

The love that the student has for his teacher is never equal to the love that the teacher has for the student, even if the spiritual teacher does not outwardly display this affection. Being aware of the spiritual teacher's love is good for the student because it brings about hope and enthusiasm. Our teacher would only use words that had a reality, and it is from this perspective that we view the words, "May I be ransomed for you," not as a mere formality, but rather as a spiritual truth.

---

person] and place him under the care of a suitable and virtuous servant so that he can then guide him to higher levels of servitude." Tahriri, p. 466.

Ayatullah Muhammad Taqi Bahjat once stated, "One who is deserving… [even] walls and doors will become his teacher, with Allah's permission." Dar Mahzar-e-Bahjat, Muhammad Husayn Rukhshad, V. 1, p. 22.

And this statement is in accordance with the Qur'anic promise that, "And as for those who strive for us, we shall surely guide them in Our ways, and Allah is indeed with the virtuous." Holy Qur'an 29:69

Humility Before the Spiritual Teacher

Ayatullah Sa'adat Parwar states, "I found it necessary to mention some matters that are useful to the wayfarer on his journey to Allah. If these are acted upon, a hundred-year path is traversed in a single year." We often approach our spiritual teachers with our own preconceived and incorrect notions about spirituality and spiritual wayfaring. For example, we say we perform this act or recite that *dhikr*.[9] In truth, we want to specify our own responsibilities, or limit the scope of our spiritual teacher's response so in the end he permits us to perform what we ourselves wanted to perform. Such conduct displays that we are oblivious to the prerequisites of this path. Those who have not traveled the path are unfamiliar with its ins-and-outs. We rely on our imaginations and what we have heard here and there. We have an incorrect understanding of spiritual wayfaring and its results, which will lead to false spirituality without any real substance.[10]

---

9. Lexically the word dhikr means to remember or remind, and its plural is adhkar. As an Islamic term it is used to refer to the words and phrases by which Almighty Allah (s) is mentioned, praised, thanked, glorified, or besought for help. In spiritual wayfaring it often refers to a specific prayer a teacher provides to a student to be recited at a particular time or in a particular manner. [Translator]

10. "How long do you wish to remain in the sleep of negligence, plunged in corruption? Fear God! Wake up from the sleep of negligence! You have not yet awakened. You have not yet taken the first step. The first step of wayfaring is awakening, but you are still asleep. Your eyes may be open, but your hearts are asleep." Combat with the Self, Khomeini, p. 31.

The valley of *Irfan*[11] is not the valley of ostentation, making noise, showiness, or saying, "Me, me, me!" From the start, the student must practice this in the presence of his spiritual teacher. It is an error for a student to suggest something in front of his spiritual teacher and to speak before listening. At times he must speak, and at times he must listen, but each has its own time and place. If we speak when we should be listening, we do not give our spiritual teacher the opportunity to take our hand and guide us. In the presence of our spiritual teacher, we should not speak out of place, but rather, we should listen more. Only with this condition did Ayatullah Sa'adat Parwar think that we could traverse 100 years in a single year.

And why shouldn't it be so?! Once one is on the path and acts in accordance with the path's requirements, he will reach his destination. Before one is on the path, there are many obstacles to reaching one's destination. However, once he begins on the path, he moves, and if he does not, he will still be taken![12] Thus, when he is in the presence of

---

11. The word Irfan comes from the same root word as arif. Linguistically the former is a verbal noun that means to know and have cognizance, while the latter is a noun for the doer, that is, the one who knows and has cognizance. However, as a term, scholars define Irfan as the name of one of the Islamic sciences that consists of two distinct parts: Theoretical Irfan, which attempts to explain the reality of existence, and Practical Irfan, which focuses on the actions one must carry out to attain proximity to Allah (s). [Translator]

12. Ayatullah Bahjat has said, "If man takes the first step on the path to earning Allah's satisfaction, the next steps will follow, and he will not

a spiritual teacher he must listen to his words and act upon them.

---

even know what happened! The first-step will pull him to places he could not have imagined." Zi-e-Talabegi, Mahdi Mutahhari, p. 35.

PART 1 – FOUNDATIONS

Etiquette 1
Obligations and Prohibitions[13]

"Perform the obligatory acts (wajibat) and avoid the prohibited ones (muharramat). After that, perform the recommended acts (mustahabat) to one's capacity and avoid the disliked acts (makruhat). From among the recommended acts, give a lot of importance to the Night Prayer (Salat al-Layl) and to wakefulness before the morning call to prayer (adhan). Also, one should not neglect performing the daily prayers at the beginning of their prescribed times, the recitation of the Holy Qur'an, and seeking the intercession of the Holy Prophet (s) and his family (a)."

---

13. Adab, translated here as Etiquette, refers to the beautification of man's actions. Imam Ali (a) said, "Indeed, Allah taught adab (etiquette) to the Messenger of Allah (s), he taught it to me, and I teach it to the believers." Mizan al-Hikmah, Muhammad Rayshahri, V. 1, p. 58.

Regarding Obligations and Prohibitions

Performing our obligations *(wajibat)* requires that we prioritize performing what Allah (s) wants over what we want. This is true even when what we want is a good action. Avoiding what is prohibited *(muharramat)* means that we abstain from whatever Allah (s) wants us to abstain from, even if we really want to perform it. Acting in this manner means overcoming the ego and not seeing oneself as primary. Sometimes we do not fully embody this mindset. For example, we pray, but without full attention. In truth, we are oblivious that praying enables us to see Allah (s) as primary, and not ourselves. If this recognition comes our prayers will improve, insha'Allah.

The first step for the wayfarer is to observe obligatory acts and to avoid prohibited acts.[14] Shame on us! Due to our ignorance we trivialize these two responsibilities. We say, "We visited our spiritual teacher, and he said nothing of substance, only to perform obligatory acts and avoid the prohibited ones." We have belittled this advice, which is the foundation of the journey towards Allah (s). The foundation of this journey is to perform the obligatory acts and to avoid what is prohibited.[15]

---

14. Ayatullah Muhammad Taqi Misbah Yazdi said, "All of the scholars of ethics among the Shia are in agreement that the path to spiritual perfection is that of obedience to the commands of Allah (s), and that there is no path other than this for one to reach high spiritual stations." Mutahhari, p. 95.
15. Prophet Musa (a) asked Khidr (a) how he reached a lofty spiritual

Your spiritual teacher has placed this special instruction in front of you, so be thankful and benefit from it. In relation to table manners, it is said that when the main course is served, eat! Do not complain and wait for something else to be served. The obligatory and prohibited acts are like the main course in that if one performs the obligatory acts and avoids the prohibited acts, he has really accomplished everything. Why do we devalue these acts? We think our spiritual teacher has not said anything substantive, so we leave our duties. After 50 years we say to ourselves, "What a shame! We wanted to grow spiritually, but we did not accomplish anything!" If we understand that this etiquette contains all of spiritual wayfaring, then our work is done.[16]

Just as wayfaring has stages, so does this etiquette. Just remember that at each stage, from the first day of wayfaring until the end of the journey, one must avoid the prohibited acts and perform the obligatory ones. This prescription is the basic element of the journey and cannot be changed; all else is secondary. O Seeker! Give attention

---

station, and Khidr (a) replied, "I abandoned sins." Tazkirat al-Mutaqeen, Bahari Hamadani, p. 53.

16. "Sin, besides its negative consequences in this world and in the hereafter, is also the cause of the existing veils between a servant and Allah (s), which deviate man such that he cannot accomplish the goal of his creation: recognizing Allah (s)." Pand Nameh-e-Sa'adat, Sa'adat Parwar, p. 26-7.

to primary matters, not secondary ones![17]

In truth, we are chasing after secondary matters when we tell our spiritual teacher, "Give me a *dhikr!*" We are attempting to specify the responsibilities our teacher should prescribe to us. Not giving importance to obligations and prohibitions is equivalent to abandoning the essential element of wayfaring to chase after secondary matters.

---

17. "It should be reiterated that from the beginning of wayfaring and spiritual journeying up to its final stage, the traveler must observe all precepts of the glorious Shari'ah, and must not violate an iota of the exoteric aspects of Divine Law…For even the Prophet (s), who was the most perfect and noblest of all creation observed all sacred precepts of the Shari'ah until the last moments of his life." Kernel of the Kernel, Concerning the Wayfaring and Spiritual Journey of the People of Intellect, Sayyid Muhammad Husayn Tabataba'i, p. 37.

Observing Recommended Acts and Avoiding What Is Disliked

"... *after that, performing the recommended acts (mustahabat) to one's capacity and avoiding the disliked acts (makruhat).*"

The philosophy of the recommended (mustahab) and disliked (makruh) actions is like that of the obligatory and prohibited ones. Allah (s) wants us to perform or avoid some acts. Allah's (s) desire for us to perform or avoid these acts is less than His desire in relation to our performing or avoiding the obligatory or prohibited ones, but His will is still there! When one observes the recommended or avoids the disliked acts, he is prioritizing Allah's (s) desires over his own, and all of wayfaring revolves around this premise. Put another way, what matters is what He says, not what we say.

Obligatory acts are prioritized over recommended acts because they have been specified by Allah (s). Our will plays no role in relation to whether we should perform the obligatory acts. However, with recommended acts Allah (s) has given us discretion as to whether we wish to perform these acts. It is from this perspective that obligatory acts are better and more effective in taking us to our destination. This is because one does not exercise even the slightest discretion in performing the obligatory acts, whereas with recommended acts, the servant's desires and discretion are still present.

Prioritizing Some Recommended Acts

Among the recommended acts, there are those that one is not necessarily inclined to perform. For example, one may be less inclined to wake up for the Night Prayer *(Salat al-Layl)* because it must be performed during what some consider to be the peak hours of sleep.[18] This is one of the reasons for the Night Prayer's special significance among the recommended acts. In the darkness of the night, those who are awake are not seen, nor do they see anyone else. This is difficult for the ego. Thus, the one who discards sleep has accomplished a difficult task. During the day, we are preoccupied and may be unable to give appropriate attention to our Lord—"For indeed during the day you have drawn-out engagements"[19]—thus, "Indeed the watch of the night is firmer in tread and more upright in respect to speech."[20] What is the speech that is being referred to in this verse? It is the Night Prayer.

---

18. Salat al-Layl consists of eleven units and can be recited between shar'i-midnight and the dawn prayer (Salat al-Fajr). Refer to the books of practical laws for more details. Imam Sadiq (a) said, "One who does not perform the Night Prayer is not one of us." Wasai'ul al-Shia, V. 7, p. 162.

قال الصادق (ع) ليس منا من لم يصل صلاة الليل

"Based on the totality of the verses of the Qur'an and ahadith... the desirability of waking up at night to perform the Night Prayer, seek forgiveness, recite Holy Qur'an, and prostrate before Allah (s) is well established..." Sirr al-Isra, Sa'adat Parwar, V. 1, p. 188.

19. Holy Qur'an 73:7 - إِنَّ لَكَ فِي النَّهَارِ سَبْحًا طَوِيلًا

20. Holy Qur'an 73:6 - إِنَّ نَاشِئَةَ اللَّيْلِ هِيَ أَشَدُّ وَطْئًا وَأَقْوَمُ قِيلًا

A spiritual teacher does not need to specify the obligatory or prohibited actions, as man himself knows their boundaries either intuitively or by way of religious texts. For example, we intrinsically know not to lie. While this matter is mentioned in our books of practical laws, we intrinsically recognize the negative aspects of lying. If you lie to me, my internal condition sufficiently displays to me the reality of such an act. Thus, prioritize avoiding prohibited actions that we would dislike had we been the victim! Have we left lying, backbiting, oppressing others, breaking promises, and other similar actions? Give priority to leaving these sins over the minutiae of the books of practical laws.

This does not mean that we do not perform obligatory acts until we have avoided all prohibited ones, but rather that avoiding prohibited acts has priority in rank and importance, not temporal priority. It does not mean that we first stop sinning and only then do we begin performing obligatory acts. Rather, start fixing those inherent and obvious shortcomings immediately. Otherwise, repeating certain adhkar or reading the prayer of Jafar al-Tayyar[21] will not place our affairs in order. Our problems are at our roots.

---

21. This prayer is considered to be the "elixir of the supplicants." Narrated with many reliable chains of narration, many virtues are attributed to it, including the forgiveness of major sins. It consists of two separate two-unit prayers, with the tasbihat al-arba'a recited 300 times in each prayer. For further details refer to Mafatih al-Jinan, Abbas Qummi, translated by Sayyid Ali Quli Qarai, V. 1 p. 124. [Translator]

1 - OBLIGATIONS & PROHIBITIONS

When performing recommended acts, remember the following four points:

1. Performing a recommended act should not harm or be an obstacle for the performance of obligatory acts.

2. Performing a recommended act should not be accompanied by a prohibited act. For example, in some mourning gatherings for Imam al-Husayn (a), some perform repulsive actions. Do not attend such gatherings.

3. One should have the physical capacity to perform the recommended act, meaning that one should not place oneself in circumstances beyond one's capacity. Being hard on ourselves and forcing ourselves to perform a recommended act can result in one being unable to perform our obligations in the best way possible.

4. One should have the spiritual disposition to perform the recommended act and should not force oneself to perform it, or one may become jaded.[22]

---

22. In this regard, Ayatullah Sa'adat Parwar quotes Allamah Tabataba'i as stating, "One who gradually advances on the path of spiritual wayfaring—and does not rush—becomes prepared for the next station of the journey." Thamarat al-Hayat, Sa'adat Parwar, V. 1, p. 105.

Imam Sadiq (a) said, "Faith has seven levels; some people are on the first level, and others on the second level… Do not place level three responsibilities on one who is on level two." Usool al-Kafi, Muhammad ibn Yacoub al-Kulayni, V. 2, p. 42.

قَالَ لَا تَحْمِلُوا عَلَى صَاحِبِ السَّهْمِ سَهْمَيْنِ وَ لَا عَلَى صَاحِبِ السَّهْمَيْنِ ثَلَاثَةً

Prioritize the Night Prayer

Ayatullah Sa'adat Parwar said, "From among the recommended acts, give a lot of attention to the Night Prayer and wakefulness before the morning *adhan*."[23] Awakening in the depths of the night is in opposition to a lazy soul. Giving into every desire one may have is not appropriate for the wayfarer. Fighting one's desires is important—even in seemingly trivial matters—when performed to train one's soul.

Note: Identifying when an act is beyond one's capacity and when someone is simply being lazy may require consultation with a spiritual teacher. [Translator]

23. Allamah Qadi said, "If you want this world, perform the Night Prayer, and if you want the next world, perform the Night Prayer." Sad Ravayat az Zindagi Ayatullah Sayyid Ali Qadi, Muhammad Jawad Meeri, p. 32.

Ustadh Muhammad Ali Mujahidi says, "Our teacher, the arif, Ayatullah Sa'adat Parwar in the last days of his life said, 'I only missed the Night Prayer once in my life, when I was unconscious due to a heart operation. Thereafter, I performed my Night Prayer Qada. If someone were to miss even one Night Prayer and not make the Qada, when they reach the next world they will be extremely upset and regretful because they will recognize what they have lost and what opportunities they gave up. Woe to one who leaves this world with more Qada Night Prayers than that!" Rahkarhay-e-Muwafaqiyat dar Tahseel-e-Uloom-e-Islami, Muhammad Ali Mujahidi, p. 78.

Imam Sadiq (a) said, "Surely one who sins will then be deprived of the Night Prayer." al-Kafi V. 2, p. 272.

عَنْ أَبِي عَبْدِ اللَّهِ ع قَالَ: إِنَّ الرَّجُلَ يُذْنِبُ الذَّنْبَ فَيُحْرَمُ صَلَاةَ اللَّيْلِ

Awakening before the morning *adhan* is important, even if one is unable to perform the Night Prayer. Wake-up and give attention to Allah (s). Some say, "I lack the spiritual disposition to perform the Night Prayer, so I do not wake up before the *adhan*." This is a mistake. For one who is starting the journey, even those few minutes that one wakes up before the morning *adhan* and sits facing the *qiblah* are important. Thereafter, he will slowly obtain the *tawfiq*[24] to perform the Night Prayer, God willing.[25]

---

[24] Tawfiq means that Allah (s) arranges causes in such a manner that they pull the servant towards the virtuous deed, or that He (s) does not bring about some of the causes that would enable the servant to perform a disobedient act. [Translator]

25. Ayatullah Muhammad Ali Shahabadi, the teacher of Imam Khomeini, stated, "If you wake up for the Night Prayer and see that you do not have the spiritual disposition to pray, stay awake! Sit down and perhaps even drink some tea. Just waking up at this time will prepare the grounds for man to worship." Arif-e-Kamil, Bunyad-e-Uloom va Maarif Islami Danish Pajuhan, p. 48.

Prioritize Praying on Time

Praying one's daily prayers at the beginning of their prescribed times is like any other invitation. If someone with a high status invites us somewhere, we accept the invitation without delay, minimizing other matters and arriving on time. Allah (s) has invited us to pray. He grants each of us a meeting with Him at the time of the *adhan* as it is then that the door to His mercy and proximity are open.

O you who constantly implore Allah (s) to open the door to His mercy and proximity! At the time of the *adhan*, the door is open, so enter! In addition, "Prayer is the ascension of the believer."[26] Thus, if one says, "I want to be a wayfarer and reach perfection," reply, "Fix your prayer." Despite this, we do not fix our prayers. We do not recite our prayers with the appropriate state and attention; neither do we practice its prerequisites, nor do we give any attention to its *adhkar* and requirements. Then we assume that if we are given an uncommon *dhikr*, it will have a greater impact?!

Imam Khomeini once said, "Prayer is the highest *dhikr* of Allah (s)." Allah (s) Himself confirms this when He

---

26. Scholars differ on whether this statement can be attributed to the Noble Messenger (s) or is a saying of the Awliya. [Translator]

Ayatullah Ansari Shirazi once said, "Whenever man stands for prayer, raises his hands, and says the Takbirat al-Ihram, the reality should be that he has disconnected his heart from the material world, has left everything, and has begun a journey in which none accompanies him other than Allah (s)." Alim-e-Rabbani, Kalam-e-Ayatullah Ansari Shirazi, p. 69.

states, "…and maintain the prayer for My remembrance."[27] We have been commanded by Allah (s) to perform this *dhikr* (the daily prayer), while many other *adhkar* have not been made obligatory. Rather than seeking unique *adhkar* from this or that person, give more attention to prayer. This includes its outward dimensions, one's attention during it, its place, and performing it at the start of its prescribed time. Fix these aspects. When Allah (s) Himself commands us to perform it, who else are we waiting for to tell us how to remember Him? Is there anything higher than the daily prayers when Allah (s) has stated, "Remember Allah with frequent remembrance…"[28]

Allah (s) states in the Holy Qur'an, "… and maintain the prayer for My remembrance."[29] We do not innately know how to remember Allah (s), so He instructs us to remember Him by way of the daily prayers. Prayer is a *dhikr* that makes man forget everything other than Allah (s) and makes Satan tremble. In spiritual wayfaring, we need to pay attention to Allah (s) and avoid Satan. Prayer is that action through which, in a single moment, we are both giving attention to the station of Allah's (s) Lordship and defying Satan. Specifically, at the start of prayer we say, "We seek refuge in Allah from Satan the Accursed."[30] Therefore,

---

27. Holy Qur'an 20:14 - إِنَّنِي أَنَا اللَّهُ لَا إِلَهَ إِلَّا أَنَا فَاعْبُدْنِي وَأَقِمِ الصَّلَاةَ لِذِكْرِي
28. Holy Qur'an 33:41 - يَا أَيُّهَا الَّذِينَ آمَنُوا اذْكُرُوا اللَّهَ ذِكْرًا كَثِيرًا
29. See Footnote 27
30. Holy Qur'an 16:98 - فَإِذَا قَرَأْتَ الْقُرْآنَ فَاسْتَعِذْ بِاللَّهِ مِنَ الشَّيْطَانِ الرَّجِيمِ

among the *adhkar*, prayer is the best *dhikr*.[31]

---

31. Allamah Qadi stated, "If someone prays his daily prayers at the beginning of their time and does not reach a high spiritual station, he can ask Allah (s) to withhold His mercy from me…If one's prayers are guarded, every other matter of theirs will remain protected." Meeri, p. 102 & 181.

Prioritize Holding Fast to the Holy Qur'an and the Ahl ul-Bayt (a)

Ayatullah Sa'adat Parwar said not to neglect the recitation of the Holy Qur'an, as the Holy Qur'an speaks to us.[32] Nor should the wayfarer neglect the seeking of intercession of the Holy Prophet (s) and his pure progeny (a). Allah (s) says, "Say, 'If you love Allah, then follow me...'"[33] The wayfarer loves Allah (s) and wishes to meet Him, so he must listen to and follow the words of the Holy Prophet (s). The loftiest, most apparent, and most precise manner to seek intercession is to follow someone. There is no benefit in one reciting *Dua al-Tawassul*[34] but not acting on the words of the Holy Messenger (s). *Dua al-Tawassul* is beneficial when it is accompanied by obedience. Hence, we should always seek intercession, but it ought to be the intercession consisting of words, remembrance, proper etiquette, and respect for the Ahl ul-Bayt (a).

Our teacher advised us to read the Holy Qur'an. What does the Holy Qur'an say about the Ahl ul-Bayt (a)?

---

32. The Holy Prophet (s) said, "The superiority of the Holy Qur'an over all other statements is akin to the superiority of Allah over his creatures." Bihar al-Anwar, Muhammad Baqir Majlisi, V. 89, p. 17.

فضل القرآن على سائر الكلام كفضل الله على خلقه

33. Holy Qur'an 3:31 - قُلْ إِن كُنتُمْ تُحِبُّونَ اللَّهَ فَاتَّبِعُونِي

34. The Supplication for Intercession (Dua al-Tawwasul) has been related by reliable sources on the authority of Muhammad b. Babawayh, who said, "I have never recited this supplication in any situation without it being answered promptly." Qummi, V. 1, p. 303.

"Indeed Allah and His angels bless the Prophet; O you who have faith! Invoke blessings on him and invoke peace upon him in a worthy manner."[35] The salutations of Allah (s) and His angels have their own unique meaning, and the salutations of people have their own unique meaning as well, but ultimately, all send salutations upon the Prophet (s). In this verse, Allah (s) states that you should send salutations "in a worthy manner." This *salawat*[36] is a *dhikr* that Allah (s) has commanded. Some say, "Give us a *dhikr!*" and when they are told to recite *salawat*, they say, "Just *salawat?!*" But, are these salutations a small thing?! Allah (s) and His angels are sending these salutations! If we are unable to send salutations in the manner that Allah (s) sends salutations—since it is not in our capacity—at the very least we can send salutations to the extent of our own capacity. Why do we think sending salutations is insignificant? If Allah (s) has commanded it, it is significant. This is the most divinely sanctioned *dhikr*.

---

35. Holy Qur'an 33:56 - إِنَّ اللَّهَ وَمَلَائِكَتَهُ يُصَلُّونَ عَلَى النَّبِيِّ يَا أَيُّهَا الَّذِينَ آمَنُوا صَلُّوا عَلَيْهِ وَسَلِّمُوا تَسْلِيمًا

36. "Salawat is the plural form of Salat which can mean 'to call'... the existence of Prophet Muhammad (s) is the first existent that came from Allah (s)...and all blessings come to the Prophet first and then to others... Thus, Allah is sending constant blessings to His Messenger and hence, the Prophet becomes rahmatun lil alamin (a mercy for the universe), and the salawat of the people on the Prophet (s) are to pray to God to send His blessings to them through the Prophet (s)." The Meaning of Salawat, Shaykh Mansour Leghaei. available at: al-islam.org/articles/meaning-salawaat-mansour-leghaei.

It is also a *dhikr* that causes no harm. It is possible that an uneducated individual instructs you to recite a *dhikr* that, rather than benefiting you, harms you.[37] The *salawat*, however, leads to no harm, as Allah (s) is pure goodness; He is "better and more lasting"[38] and He commands us to do good.[39] Thus, since He commanded us to recite the *salawat*, the *salawat* is pure goodness.

Furthermore, reciting the *salawat* is acting upon a Qur'anic Truth, and only by acting in accordance with Qur'anic precepts can one manifest the reality of the Qur'an. For example, the Qur'an states, "Do not exact usury…"[40] If we recite this verse, but continue charging others interest, we are far away from this Qur'anic reality. To reach the Truth, we must begin by performing what the Qur'an says to perform and avoiding what it prohibits.

The Holy Qur'an states, "…Invoke blessings on him and invoke peace upon him in a worthy manner."[41] This action moves us toward the reality of the Qur'an. It

---

37. When treating a physical illness we understand that not all medications or dosages are appropriate for all individuals and circumstances. Similarly, when treating a spiritual illness not all adhkar are appropriate for all individuals or circumstances. [Translator]

38. Holy Qur'an 20:73 - وَاللَّهُ خَيْرٌ وَأَبْقَىٰ

39. Imam Ali (a) said, "Do good and do not underestimate it at all, for verily a little good is actually a lot…" Nahjul Balagha, Saying 422.

40. Holy Qur'an 3:130 - يَا أَيُّهَا الَّذِينَ آمَنُوا لَا تَأْكُلُوا الرِّبَا أَضْعَافًا مُضَاعَفَةً وَاتَّقُوا اللَّهَ لَعَلَّكُمْ تُفْلِحُونَ

41. Holy Qur'an 33:56 - إِنَّ اللَّهَ وَمَلَائِكَتَهُ يُصَلُّونَ عَلَى النَّبِيِّ يَا أَيُّهَا الَّذِينَ آمَنُوا صَلُّوا عَلَيْهِ وَسَلِّمُوا تَسْلِيمًا

is an important, albeit simple, action. The *salawat* is one of those *adhkar* that every Muslim can recite young or old, educated or uneducated, marja or laborer. There is no apparent ostentation, showing-off, or *riya*[42] in performing this act, and since we are afflicted with *riya*, those acts that do not open the door to *riya* are extremely beneficial for us. For example, commemorating the Master of the Martyrs, Imam al-Husayn (a), is an act that does not provide much opportunity for *riya*. In the case of the *salawat*, along with the fact that there is no apparent *riya*, it is said that whoever recites this supplication loudly, his self-conceit (*kibr*) will be annihilated. Since the wayfarer is seeking to annihilate his self-conceit and become humble, the *salawat* is the best *dhikr* for the wayfarer.

Intercession can be viewed through various lenses, such as thinking about the infallible, visiting the infallible, pleading to the infallible, or by way of obedience, which is the best lens.[43] Thereafter, one should focus on the recitation

---

42. "Riya means to falsely make oneself appear to be virtuous, good natured, or a true believer in God before the people for the sake of earning their respect and admiration or gaining a good reputation among them." Forty Hadith, An Exposition of Ethical and Mystical Traditions, Sayyid Ruhollah Khomeini, p. 57.

Imam Sadiq (a) has said, "Riya, in any of its forms, amounts to shirk (polytheism); verily, one who works for the people, his reward lies with them, and one who works for God, his reward lies with God." Kulayni, V. 2, p. 402.

43. Imam Muhammad Baqir (a) said, "Is it sufficient for one who claims to be our Shia to state that he loves us?! I swear by God that our Shia are

of the *salawat*, and supplications that include intercession, such as *Dua al-Tawassul*. The Holy Prophet (s) and his pure progeny (a) have commanded us not to leave this and other ziyarat and supplications until the end of our lives. Actually, it is through these supplications that we are given life, and the life of the wayfarer is these very supplications.

This was the first etiquette that Ayatullah Sa'adat Parwar advised the wayfarer to abide by if he wishes to traverse 100 years in a single year.

---

only those who fear Allah (s) and are obedient to Him." Tuhaf al-Uqool, Ibn Shu'ba, p. 295.

ما شِيَعَتُنا إلاّ مَنِ اتَّقَى اللهَ و أطاعَهُ

Etiquette 2
Attending to a Teacher

"Attend to a spiritual teacher and act upon his statements. Relate all states (halat), stations (maqamat), visions (mushahadat), and even dreams encountered. Do not present your own view in relation to the teacher's view on spiritual wayfaring."

Attending to a Spiritual Teacher[44]

The word insan (human) is from the root ن س ي (to forget) or أ ن س (to come to know). In either case, the nature of man is that he is afflicted with forgetfulness. We require constant reminders, otherwise we are sometimes mindful of Allah (s), and sometimes we are inattentive.[45] Being in such a state will not resolve our spiritual problems. As the poem goes: "Five things make the incomplete ones complete: silence, hunger, night vigil, solitude, and steady remembrance keep."[46] One who has been inattentive to Allah (s) cannot suddenly become consistently attentive on his or her own. A change in one's nature requires a cause.

Among the causes of the remembrance of Allah (s) is one's spiritual teacher. The more one is attached to his spiritual teacher, their remembrance of Allah (s) increases.

---

44. "The teacher, who is necessary for all but the first stages of wayfaring, will possess the following characteristics: firstly, he will be aware of the fundamental teachings of the Qur'an and the Sunnah; secondly, he will have traversed this path, and a portion of the tawhidi realms will have been unveiled for him; thirdly, he will be capable of helping and training those who are deserving." Tahriri, p. 234.
45. "Since man is inclined to forget and become ignorant, absolutely no one should consider themselves needless of reminders." Risaleh-e-Irfani, Sa'adat Parwar, p. 201.
46. This line of poetry is often attributed to Sayyid Muhammad Jawad Sadr Amuli. Another variation is attributed to Shah Qasim Anwar. See Treatise on Spiritual Journeying and Wayfaring attributed to Bahr al-Uloom, annotated by Sayyid Muhammad Husayn Husayni Tihrani, p. 233.

If the wayfarer is attached to his teacher, the teacher will make the path forward smooth, creating a constancy of remembrance within the wayfarer. This does not happen immediately as the teacher does not transform the wayfarer instantaneously.

Being attached to a teacher is not necessarily a physical matter. It may be that the wayfarer does not visit his teacher in person. Sometimes it is the case that there is a physical distance between the teacher and the wayfarer and it becomes impossible for the wayfarer to consistently visit his teacher. Therefore, the relationship must be such that both the physically-near and the physically-distant wayfarer are able to attend to their teacher and benefit accordingly. If the attending and attachment are physical, all the better. If not, a spiritual attachment is sufficient. After all, this is a journey, and the primary meaning of "attending" or "attachment" to a teacher is to act on his advice.

One should not precede one's teacher, but rather should travel alongside him as a companion. This companionship is the result of a close attachment. If the attachment to one's teacher is only physical, meaning that the wayfarer simply sits and socializes with this teacher but does not follow his instructions, there is no benefit. Attachment to a teacher without following his instructions will have no effect, even if the teacher is the Final Messenger (s) or Imam Ali (a).[47]

---

47. Along these lines Ayatullah Bahjat has said, "No student should look

2 - ATTENDING TO A TEACHER

Many people sat with the Holy Prophet (s) and Imam Ali (a), but there is now a great distance between them and these holy personalities. Some of those who attended to these great personalities are at the highest of stations while others are not. Therefore, the basis of attachment to one's teacher is to follow him, and the more serious one is in this matter—without falling into extremes—the better. It is this attachment that will deliver man to perfection.

In the *Salawat al-Shabaniyya* we read, "O Allah, bless Muhammad and the family of Muhammad, the ark faring through deep oceans. Those who embark upon it obtain safety and those who forsake it are drowned."[48] This ark is constantly moving forward through difficult waves, not sitting idle. Similarly, the wayfarer will face difficult waves on his journey and will be in danger of drowning and thus requires an ark. "Those who embark upon it obtain safety and those who forsake it are drowned."[49] One who boards this ark will traverse his journey in safety. It is not that he will sit safely without difficulties, rather, he will be in difficulties, but he will overcome them.

A question that comes to mind here is how does one

---

at his teacher [and therefore assume that he is going to heaven]. Man should look at his own actions [when considering his final-destination]." Mutahhari, p. 98.

48. اللهم صل على محمد و آل محمد الفلك الجارية في اللجج الغامرة يأمن من ركبها و يغرق Salawat of Sha'ban, من تركها المتقدم لهم مارق و المتأخر عنهم زاهق و اللازم لهم لاحق Qummi, V. 1, p. 421.

49. Ibid.

board the ark? "Those who advance ahead of them leave the bounds of faith…"[50] If the Holy Prophet (s) or the Imam (a) say one thing, and then someone selects something else for themselves, that is the definition of disbelief even if one beautifully professes faith on the apparent level. One will not reach the purpose of existence with such conduct. The wayfarer must be attached to Islam. Someone who does not adhere to the statements of the Ahl al-Bayt (a) will fall behind and drown in falsehood:"…and those who lag behind them perish…"[51] Only those who are attached to the Ahl al-Bayt (a) will reach the truth and realities:"…and those who attach themselves to them join their fold."[52]

In summary, accompanying one's teacher means that one should not proceed or lag behind him, but rather travel alongside him in order to see what he says and how he acts. Ayatullah Sa'adat Parwar said to "act on his statements…" which is part and parcel of attending to one's teacher, and this is one of the most basic principles of this path.

---

50. Ibid.
51. Ibid.
52. Ibid.

The Teacher's Authority

Understanding the extent of a spiritual teacher's authority should be resolved at the start of the student-teacher relationship.[53] The wayfarer should select a teacher he believes can lead him on the path to perfection.[54] A real teacher does not force a student into anything. At the same time, a teacher will be limited if he needs to provide proof or an explanation for every matter. If a teacher knows he will not be questioned about everything he says, he can more effectively guide his student. For example, there is a recommended act that one wishes to perform, but the spiritual teacher says not to perform it. If the wayfarer's red-lines in relation to his teacher's instructions are the

---

53. "[A student] should prioritize selecting a teacher with the best character, spirituality, and taqwa, even if the teacher is lesser in knowledge than others." Mujahadi, p. 63.

54. "[A spiritual master] cannot be identified except through intimate association with him in public and private. A wayfarer should observe him and verify the perfection of faith in his limbs (outwardly) and in his soul (inwardly). One should be warned not to be deceived into following someone because of seeing him performing supernatural acts, discussing subtleties, revealing cosmic mysteries, disclosing personal secrets, or changing some of his circumstances. One can read minds, discover subtleties, walk on water, teleport through the air and land, foretell the future, and do other similar acts, all at the stage of spiritual unveiling. There is an infinitely long way from this stage to the final-destination and the completion of the journey. There are yet numerous stations and stages to pass. Many travelers have passed this stage but strayed later, ending up with the thieves and devils of the path. This is how some disbelievers have been able to do certain miraculous acts." Treatise attributed to Bahr al-Uloom, p. 82.

obligatory and prohibited actions, as it should be, he will act on this instruction. Doubting such instructions will be harmful to the wayfarer, and he will not reach perfection.

Obedience to and following one's spiritual teacher are voluntary acts. They were conditional from the start and are compatible with the *shariah*. It is not possible to state, "I am ready, but my opinion is this!" No one told you to come to the gym, but if you come, wear your shoes. If you say you want to come barefoot, we will stop you. If you have voluntarily come to the gym, wear the footwear specified for the gym or you will not reach your intended goal.

Sharing Your Spiritual Condition

Ayatullah Sa'adat Parwar said, "...relating all states *(halat)*, stations *(maqamat)*, and visions *(mushahadat)*..."[55] For the wayfarer, spiritual states will come, and once established they are referred to as stations. Sometimes one may see things that we refer to as visions. Do any of these matters have any value? In and of themselves, these *halat*, *maqamat*, and *mushahadat* have no value, meaning that if a spiritual state arises and results in one thinking good of oneself, he has, in reality, become attached to the wrong thing. Giving undue attention to these matters is far from the path.[56] Human capacity is higher than to give

---

55. Shahid Murtadha Mutahhari defines a hal (state) as a spiritual condition that descends upon someone for a limited time without their will, whereas a maqam (station) is earned and remains constant. See Kalam, Irfan, Hikmat-e-Amali, Shaheed Murtadha Mutahhari, p. 154. As for an example of a mushahada (vision), Allamah Hasan Hasanzadeh Amuli narrates that in the year 1387 AH (1968 AD) at the time of the Dhuhr prayer, he saw two figures in his room. One was reciting the adhan in a beautiful voice, but appeared and disappeared such that Allamah was unable to recognize him. Allamah questioned the other figure about who was reciting this adhan and was told that it was the Noble Messenger, Muhammad al-Mustafa (s). Insan dar Urf-e-Irfan, Allamah Hasan Hasanzadeh Amuli, p. 31.

56. A student of Allamah Qadi narrates: "One night I was having trouble awakening for the Night Prayer when a beautiful angel appeared before me. This resulted in me rising and performing the Night Prayer. I related this event to Sayyid Ali Qadi who said, 'Strange! You are still attached to forms. When will you reach deeper truths?!' Sayyid Ali Qadi would not give attention to visions and extraordinary feats that would come about on the path of spiritual wayfaring. He would add, 'Do not allow the desire

importance to such matters, which, at times, are themselves obstacles. It is as if one is on a trip but is sidetracked by some food that he encounters on the journey and thus does not reach his destination.

Therefore, *halat, maqamat,* and *mushahadat* can be obstacles. If one experiences any of these, he should not give them undue attention such that they become objects of worship and obstacles to continuing on the path towards Allah (s). Rather, they are gifts so that one becomes hopeful in continuing the journey. It is also possible that they include information to assist a person on the journey. From this perspective, it is good for the wayfarer to share these matters with his spiritual teacher, who understands them and can explain them accordingly. For example, a particular dream may communicate a particular state or characteristic in you that requires attention.

When we say relate your dreams or *halat* to your spiritual teacher, it does not mean to share all of their intricate details. Rather, share the crux of the matter and relevant details. We often recognize what is important and what deserves to be shared with our spiritual teacher. For example, one dreams that he constantly wishes to pray, but he is unable to go into *ruku*, or his *qiblah* is crooked, or other similar matters. It is good for the wayfarer to share these details with his spiritual teacher so that he understands the wayfarer's defects and shortcomings and can caution him.

---

for heaven to make you negligent of the Creator of heaven!'" Meeri, p. 47.

Sometimes we go to our spiritual teacher and describe a dream or state and ask him to tell us our defects or shortcomings, but we begin to give our own opinions and explanations. Our teacher does not object to our conduct so as not to hurt our feelings or lessen our eagerness. It is not in his disposition to interrupt or silence us, so he listens. But know that for a wayfarer to act in this manner is far from the path. Be all ears when approaching your teacher.

A wayfarer should share the main points of his states, visions, and dreams with his spiritual teacher. These matters help the spiritual teacher understand the student and what instructions are appropriate for him. A wayfarer should not specify or suggest a duty to the spiritual teacher and state, for example, "Should I say this *dhikr* or that one? Share the necessary information with your spiritual teacher, and if he sees benefit in a particular act, he will advice you based upon your capacity. Sometimes we have reached the conclusion that such-and-such action is good for us, and we just want to hear our own conclusion come from our teacher's mouth. When you go to your teacher, remember the following: "In love's fold of talking and hearing, one cannot boast; for there, all thy limbs must be just eyes and ears. In the circle of subtlety-knowers, it is not proper to praise oneself, O man of wisdom! Utter weighed words or be silent!"[57]

---

57. Divan of Hafiz.

Etiquette 3
Being Balanced

"Avoid [the extremes of] excessiveness and deficiency in every matter."

Observe Moderation

Imam Ali (a) said, "You will only find an ignorant person in one of two states: either in a state of excess or deficiency."[58] Being excessive or deficient are the keys to ignorance. Man works in this world to get his reward in the hereafter. If he is performing ritual acts of worship *(ibadah)*, he should know that these acts should not become obstacles to performing his other responsibilities.[59] For example, one of man's responsibilities is to attend to his family, and ritual acts of worship should not be an obstacle to this. It is wrong for someone to leave his family and say, "They have Allah (s), He will attend to them Himself!" It is true that they have Allah (s), but He has entrusted them to your care! Neglecting one's family to perform ritual acts of worship or to recite *adhkar* results in those very acts of worship having no spiritual impact. This is because Allah (s) does not desire for you to perform ritual acts of worship that are not your duty, at the expense of your other duties.[60]

---

58. Nahjul Balagha, Saying 70.
59. "Avoid the extremes of excessiveness and deficiency in matters of ritual worship. Perform these acts in relation to your spiritual disposition, unless they are obligatory acts and the time to perform the action is limited…" Risaleh-e-Irfani, Sa'adat Parwar, p. 194.
60. The Holy Prophet (s) said, "A man sitting beside his family is more beloved to Allah (s) than a man spending the night in worship in this mosque of mine." Rayshahri, V. 5 p. 101. عنه صلى الله عليه و آله : جُلوسُ المَرءِ عندَ عِيالِهِ أَحَبُّ إلى اللهِ تعالى مِنِ اعتِكافٍ في مَسجِدي هذا

Perform Your Duty

Performing one's duty or obligation is equivalent to being occupied with the worship of Allah (s) and is giving attention to Allah (s). One who ignores his responsibilities and instead chases after excessive ritual acts of worship is actually chasing after and worshiping his own desires.[61] When man performs his duties, he is stating, "My Lord, for the sake of that which You like, I have abstained from many acts that I like," and this is the very basis of worship.

Man's duty is to not display excessiveness or deficiency in ritual acts of worship or any other matter. Man's duty is to perform the moderate amount that Allah (s) has specified for every matter. One who performs more or less than what is expected is not pleasing Allah (s), and such conduct is inconsistent with the basis of servitude and spiritual wayfaring.[62]

---

61. Ustadh Mujahidi relates, "I knew a scholar who worked hard for the Revolution and was even imprisoned during the time of the Shah. After the Revolution he slowly lost the path and eventually moved abroad and assisted foreign powers. I asked my teacher Ayatullah Sa'adat Parwar why this individual lost the path. He replied that the scholar went to extremes performing ritual acts of worship during his early years as a seminary student, acts beyond his capacity." Mujahidi, p. 90.

62. "In view of the recommendations of the Imams (a), the wayfarers of the path towards Allah (s)—those who wish to set out on this path and achieve its spiritual results—must act firstly with leniency and moderation and secondly with a constant and lasting practical routine." Tahriri, p. 489.

Ayatullah Sa'adat Parwar recommended that his students eat and sleep an appropriate amount and not fall into extremes in this regard. See Pand Nameh-e-Sa'adat, Sa'adat Parwar, p. 28-9.

PART 2 – FRATERNITY

Etiquette 4
Where Do You Sit?

"Avoid listening to speech that distracts and divides one's attention. In addition, avoid sitting with those who are careless with their speech and actions, even if they are wayfarers."

Avoid Listening to Useless Speech

Man perceives what is around him by way of his senses. The Holy Qur'an states, "Allah has brought you forth from the bellies of your mothers while you did not know anything. He made for you hearing, eyesight, and hearts so that you may give thanks."[63] Many of man's perceptions are obtained through his ears. From the beginning of life, the newborn is sensitive to noise; if he hears something from one direction, he turns his head. We know that the child perceives sound, otherwise he would not turn his head, laugh, feel comforted by the sound of his mother's voice, or cry when he hears a loud noise.

The ear has two functions: to hear and to listen. Whereas hearing is the automatic function of the ear – man hears even the unwanted sounds that reach his ear- listening stems from man's will. Both hearing and listening can change one's state. One can grow, transcend, fall into decadence, find solace, or become disturbed by way of these two functions. And, although we said that hearing happens without our will, we often can still control what we hear. For example, we can avoid being in certain places, thus controlling what we hear, even if not completely.

Listening, however, is a conscious decision and is therefore within our control as we can either choose to

---

63. Holy Qur'an, 16:78 - وَاللّٰهُ أَخْرَجَكُم مِّن بُطُونِ أُمَّهَاتِكُمْ لَا تَعْلَمُونَ شَيْئًا وَجَعَلَ لَكُمُ السَّمْعَ وَالْأَبْصَارَ وَالْأَفْئِدَةَ لَعَلَّكُمْ تَشْكُرُونَ

listen or choose not to listen. The Holy Prophet (s) came "to purify them and to teach them the Book."[64] What was their response? "...they would put their fingers into their ears,"[65] and say, "Do not listen to this Qur'an, and hoot it down..."[66] They interrupted his speech and separated themselves from him. On the other hand, there were those who came from far-away lands and said, "Advise me!" Such people placed their ears at the authority of the Holy Prophet (s). Thus, hearing and listening are important and are often within our control. What is perceived by way of the sense of hearing can be repulsive or beautiful; it can guide or misguide. Children perceive more from the sense of hearing than any other route, and this is their state until they mature.

The Holy Qur'an states in relation to heaven, "They will not hear therein any vain talk or sinful speech..."[67] and "...wherein they will not hear any vain talk."[68] A characteristic of heaven is that man's perceptions are positive and divine: nonsense does not exist there. Thus, if we desire to be deserving of heaven, we should obtain such characteristics here.

We cannot be attached to useless matters and still reach perfection! We must create an environment for

---

64. Holy Qur'an, 3:164 - وَيُزَكِّيهِمْ وَيُعَلِّمُهُمُ الْكِتَابَ وَالْحِكْمَةَ
65. Holy Qur'an, 71:7 - جَعَلُوا أَصَابِعَهُمْ فِي آذَانِهِمْ
66. Holy Qur'an, 41: 26 - لَا تَسْمَعُوا لِهَٰذَا الْقُرْآنِ وَالْغَوْا فِيهِ لَعَلَّكُمْ تَغْلِبُونَ
67. Holy Qur'an, 56:25 - لَا يَسْمَعُونَ فِيهَا لَغْوًا وَلَا تَأْثِيمًا
68. Holy Qur'an, 88:11 - لَا تَسْمَعُ فِيهَا لَاغِيَةً

ourselves such that frivolous matters do not reach our ears. What you hear impacts the heart. When the heart becomes selective of what it should and should not hear, it is prepared for spiritual elevation, and becomes capable of distinguishing good from bad and right from wrong. However, if we allow ourselves to hear frivolous and harmful sounds, our hearts become darkened. How refreshing is it for one constantly engulfed in smoke to visit the mountains and get some fresh air? The same is true for one's heart; pleasant sounds and speech refresh the heart, whereas frivolous and inconsequential speech have the opposite effect.

The Wayfarer's Relationships

We must regulate what we hear and listen to so that our hearts remain immaculate and pure. Frequenting gatherings with careless people places our hearts in harm's way. Careless people are those who speak without thinking, speak ill of others, backbite, insult, tell lies, and speak about useless matters.

Even if a good person or a wayfarer mentions such matters, do not give him your attention. Irrelevant speech will affect us, and it makes no difference from whom we heard the indecent speech. Perhaps hearing such speech from a wayfarer makes us think that there is no problem in it because it was said by so-and-so, but this is not the case. Notably, when wayfarers gather, their conversations should differ from those of [heedless people].

If man is habituated to indecent or careless speech, it becomes part of his nature. Thereafter, speaking in accordance with Islamic etiquette will no longer be enjoyable or acceptable to him. The ears of the heart should be able to appreciate *"La ilaaha illa Allah."*[69] When the sounds of *takbir* *(Allahu Akbar)* or praise of Allah (s) reach the heart, they should influence the heart. If the heart becomes habituated

---

69. Meaning: There is no deity worthy of worship except Allah (s). The two testimonies (Shahadatayn) testify to the Oneness of Allah (s) and the prophethood of Muhammad (s). One who testifies to these two truths enters the fold of Islam and is a Muslim. [Translator]

to useless and frivolous matters, *"La ilaaha illa Allah"* becomes a strange thing. It is a *dhikr* that, upon reaching the hearts, ought to cause them to tremble.[70] *"La ilaaha illa Allah"* is the remembrance of Allah and if it does not impact someone, it is because their heart is accustomed to listening to useless matters.

A person whose heart has no real connection to *adhkar* will not gain pleasure from them, understand their depths, enjoy their recitation, or gain intimacy with them. What we hear is extremely important and we should give attention to this truth. We mistakenly believe that we can hear or listen to whatever we like and someday rectify our condition. It will be too late.

It is for this very reason that it has been said, "Do not sit at the foot of every pulpit" and "Do not listen to every speech." It is narrated that Imam Muhammad Jawad (a) has said, "The one who listens to a speaker worships him: Thus, if the speaker speaks about Allah, he has worshiped Allah, and if the speaker speaks in the tongue of Satan, he has worshiped Satan."[71] The listener entrusts his ear to the speaker; it is not simply that someone spoke and we listened. No! Speech impacts the heart, and one should not

---

70. Holy Qur'an, 8:2 - إِنَّمَا الْمُؤْمِنُونَ الَّذِينَ إِذَا ذُكِرَ اللَّهُ وَجِلَتْ قُلُوبُهُمْ وَإِذَا تُلِيَتْ عَلَيْهِمْ آيَاتُهُ زَادَتْهُمْ إِيمَانًا وَعَلَىٰ رَبِّهِمْ يَتَوَكَّلُونَ

71. مَنْ أَصْغَى إِلَى نَاطِقٍ فَقَدْ عَبَدَهُ فَإِنْ كَانَ النَّاطِقُ عَنِ اللَّهِ فَقَدْ عَبَدَ اللَّهَ و إِنْ كَانَ النَّاطِقُ يَنْطِقُ عَنْ لِسَانِ إِبْلِيسَ فَقَدْ عَبَدَ إِبْلِيسَ Mustadrak al-Wasail, Muhadith Nuri, V. 17, p. 308.

worship Satan. If we have been told not to listen to everyone and everything, it is not to restrict us. Rather, it is to ensure the purity of our hearts.

This fourth etiquette is extremely important. The mind of the wayfarer is after unity—"there is no God except Him"[72]—however, divergent words bring about division and disharmony in the heart. Ayatullah Sa'adat Parwar advised us to avoid contact with those who are "careless in their words and deeds, even if they are wayfarers." This is an extremely important etiquette, and the wayfarer will even reach a rank where he will consider this matter to be close to obligatory on himself.

Sometimes we say to ourselves that so-and-so came to a gathering and made a comment, if only he had not! A wayfarer, however, should reach a rank where if he sits in such a gathering, he will censure himself and not others, saying, "Why did I attend this gathering?!" Thereafter, he will be more careful about attending such a gathering. The statement, "The good deeds of the righteous are the sins of those brought closest to Allah," points to this truth.[73] In truth, some speech lacks benefit, as more attention is being given to trivial matters than necessary. For example, suppose one poses the question: "Who had a higher spiritual rank,

---

72. Holy Qur'an, 2:163 - وَإِلَٰهُكُمْ إِلَٰهٌ وَاحِدٌ لَا إِلَٰهَ إِلَّا هُوَ الرَّحْمَٰنُ الرَّحِيمُ
73. حَسَنَاتُ الْأَبْرَارِ سَيِّئَاتُ الْمُقَرَّبِينَ
Bihar al-Anwar, V. 25, p. 205, attributed to the Holy Messenger (s). Others attribute this statement to the Awliya.

Ayatullah Bahjat or Allamah Tabataba'i?" This question is totally irrelevant to us and holds no real value. And even if we assume such a question is relevant, it should be posed to someone capable of answering it!

Such conversations do not add value to our gatherings and mentally preoccupy us. We ponder over such matters when we have not even taken the preliminary steps to avoid the prohibited actions or to perform our obligations. We want to compare the spiritual methodology of this teacher to that teacher. Such discussions raise doubts and confusion in people's minds and are not beneficial. The wayfarer should not investigate matters that unnecessarily preoccupy him.

Ayatullah Sa'adat Parwar would not allow our gatherings to reach such a state. Rather, after exchanging pleasantries, he would place a book of *ahadith* before one of the attendees and instruct him to read. In that way, we would learn something and would not start talking about whatever we desired. Usually in such gatherings after exchanging pleasantries, people say, "So, what's up?" and after this question the conversation degenerates. Thus, from the start of our gatherings our spiritual teacher would act as an obstacle to this phenomenon. We would recite a *hadith* so that our attention would not be diverted and so that our hearts would not be harmed. A wayfarer can then perform his duties without unnecessary mental preoccupations.

Etiquette 5
Friends of the Path

"Interacting with a self-vigilant wayfarer is very good. However, if he holds peculiar beliefs regarding the affairs of wayfaring, then only take into consideration that which your teacher instructs otherwise it will create divisiveness [and result in a wasted opportunity]."

The Basis of Friendship

A wayfarer is tested by way of his friendships. Through friendships one can see whether he is still primarily concerned with himself. If he is not tested, he will not become an elite and seasoned wayfarer. By way of friends, a wayfarer is tested, consulted, and sacrifices. If these actions are performed for the sake of Allah (s), the wayfarer will love his friend for the sake of Allah (s) as well. Thus, he bears his friend's burdens and seriously attends to him during his difficulties, sicknesses, and hardships. On the path of spiritual wayfaring if one is attentive to the needs of others, the selfish ego recedes accordingly.

Friendships based on worldly considerations are often based upon selfish expectations and desires. We sometimes hear statements like: "He only comes to me when he needs something!" or, "When has he ever helped me?!" or, "Did you visit even once to see how I was doing while I was sick?" The wayfarer does not have such expectations from his friends; rather, he is the opposite—he sacrifices himself for his friends.[74]

---

74. Imam Ali (a) said, "A sincere friend is he who advises you regarding your shortcomings, protects you in your absence, and prefers you over himself." Rayshahri, hadith 1904.

قال علي (ع): الصديق من نصحك في عيبك و حفظك في غيبك و آثارك على نفسك

Friends of the Path

That which assists and benefits the wayfarer on this path is having a friend who is a fellow wayfarer. For example, when one wayfarer interacts with another, it decreases his need to interact with those unfamiliar with this path. Similarly, a wayfaring friend is helpful when one encounters difficulties related to his beliefs or actions.

However, a wayfaring friend should not hold any misguided beliefs that would be costly for the wayfarer. For example, Allah (s) states about the Prophet (s): "Nor does he speak out of [his own] desire: it is just a revelation that is revealed [to him]."[75] If a person does not fully accept this verse and instead is one of those "enlightened" individuals who believe that the Prophet (s) committed errors and can be criticized, his wayfaring friend will be ruined. Do not take the existence of such wrong beliefs lightly, as such a person will create headaches for a wayfarer.

One must have sorted out such fundamental issues prior to having embarked upon spiritual wayfaring. It should not be that once on the path, one still questions, for example, how is it that the Imam of the Time (a.f.) knows our pains? How would he understand 100 people speaking to him in 100 languages? For someone with such fundamental questions, wayfaring is premature. One should first sort out these questions. A friend who consistently introduces

---

75. Holy Qur'an, 53:3-4 -وَمَا يَنطِقُ عَنِ ٱلْهَوَىٰ إِنْ هُوَ إِلَّا وَحْيٌ يُوحَىٰ

doubts and asks odd questions preoccupies the wayfarer, and gradually darkness will envelop the wayfarer's heart. What should a wayfarer do with such a friend? Should he debate his friend, or not? If he debates him, perhaps he is wasting time on a trivial matter. If he does not debate him, the friend will remain on his incorrect view and will take the wayfarer's silence as implicit confirmation of his incorrect beliefs.

Discussions and debates related to such matters often end in dispute. For example, you want to prove to your friend that criticizing the Holy Prophet (s) is absurd, as he is the supreme representative and the vicegerent of Allah (s). The names and characteristics of Allah (s) have been taught to him, and by Allah's (s) permission the Holy Prophet (s) embodies these traits. Thus, the words of all humans and jinn, in whatever language or dialect, can be understood by the Prophet (s), and he even understands the call of a tiny ant. Your friend replies, "Those traditions were only made to convey that the Prophet (s) or Imam (a) is knowledgeable. Who can understand the speech of an ant?!" Such a friend is not beneficial for a wayfarer, as he creates distractions rather than bringing about the peace of mind necessary for spiritual wayfaring.

We sometimes socialize with friends thinking that we are all headed in the same direction, but what if this is not the case? Imagine if there were ten people pushing a car, but four of them were pushing it in the opposite direction of the other six. These four would neutralize the efforts of four of those on the other side and there would not be enough strength to accomplish the task. Thus, if even a few people in a gathering for spiritual training consistently debate and raise unfounded criticisms, the gathering will not benefit anyone. Sometimes such individuals raise theological doubts that require an entire class on theology to resolve. When it comes to spiritual wayfaring, however, these discussions are neither appropriate nor relevant; rather, they bring about disharmony.[76]

---

76. It should be noted that asking a qualified scholar about one's legitimate questions or doubts related to subjects such as monotheism, Islam, philosophy, law, history. is encouraged and is one of the keys to growth and reaching certainty of faith. The questioning being discouraged here is in relation to a gathering for spiritual training, where it is understood that one has already accepted the basic tenets of Islam and the authority of a qualified spiritual master. Such a gathering has a specific purpose that will not be reached if inundated with theological questions. [Translator]

The Role of a Friend

When our spiritual teacher would advise us not to pay attention to any special instructions other than the special instructions he prescribed, we would listen. A friend on the path may mention something that is not in accordance with what one's own spiritual teacher prescribes. Acting on such advice causes disharmony and is not beneficial for the wayfarer. But a friend on the path can strengthen the wayfarer and keep him away from laziness. For example, his help ensures that one performs his Night Prayer, or is not inclined to sin or towards the love of this world. If one has a friend like this, he should sacrifice himself for such a friend; he should give his own food and spend his own wealth on such a friend. However, if this friend has misguided beliefs in relation to wayfaring or theology, he is an affliction, not a friend. We pray that Allah (s) does not ordain such a friend for us!

Etiquette 6
Ahl al-Dunya

"Interacting with worldly people (ahl al-dunya)[77] and those who only care about eating and sleeping, and going here-and-there, is harmful, except to the extent that it is necessary."

---

77. The word dunya literally refers to something that is low or close by. This world is referred to as the dunya because of its lowliness when compared to the hereafter and the higher realms of existence. Ayatullah Jawadi Amuli, quoting the Holy Qur'an (3:14), says, "Nobility is not to be found within the confines and conventions of this mundane world. Whatever carries the flavor of this world is definitely not the source of nobility. In fact, it is the root of baseness." Nobility in the Qur'an, Abdullah Jawadi Amuli, p. 18.

Avoid Interacting with Worldly People

The wayfarer is after the truth, meaning that he is after Allah (s), and other than Allah (s), nothing is real. The wayfarer is traveling toward the afterlife, which is the truth. This world has no reality compared to the afterlife, which is itself the inner reality of this world. Worldly people are those who are satisfied with the apparent world, which obstructs man from the truth and esoteric realities. It is inconceivable that someone can be worldly and reach truth and inner realities at the same time. In a system based on causality, one reaches what he struggles for. One does not struggle to reach a certain goal and then reach an entirely different goal. For example, if one travels from Chicago to Detroit, he should not expect to reach Los Angeles.

Worldly people pursue and reach only the material matters of this world, while they are uninterested in reaching the deeper truths related to Allah (s) or the hereafter. If a wayfarer accompanies a worldly person, their companionship necessitates that they travel on the same path and in the same direction. Interacting with people—whatever their persuasion—inclines one to that persuasion, and this is because the lowly world is deceitful. As Imam Ali (a) states in *Nahjul Balagha*, "The dunya deceives, damages, and then leaves."[78] The dunya does not fall for your tricks, unless you are from the elite friends of Allah (s), who rub

---

78. الدُّنْيَا تَغُرُّ وَ تَضُرُّ وَ تَمُرُّ Nahjul Balagha, Saying 415.

the nose of the lowly world into the ground. Otherwise, this lowly world deceives man and then leaves, and only loss remains with us.

Among the damages left behind is the incapability to travel on the spiritual path. The damage inflicted by the lowly world does not mean that we lose our houses, cars, or lives. Rather, this lowly world takes Allah (s) and the afterlife from us and drowns us in its apparent formalities. In this way, worldly people view these formalities as progress and gallop toward them, taking whoever travels with them along for the ride, like a flood sweeping everything in its path. The remedy is to limit our interactions with those who are wordly because increasing our interactions with them will result in us resembling them in goal and action. It has been said, "Tell me who your friends are, and I'll tell you who you are." If all of your friends are worldly people, you likely are too, so be careful not to frequent such friends.[79]

Do not say, "I frequently socialize with worldly people, but I am still attentive to Allah (s)." This is impossible. The lowly world is so charming that very few escape it unharmed. Therefore, it is better for one to be attentive from the start. As Saadi said, "The source of a fountain may be stopped with a spade, but when it is full it cannot be

---

79. "So avoid those who turn away from Our remembrance and desire nothing but the life of the world." Holy Qur'an 53:29
فَأَعْرِضْ عَن مَّن تَوَلَّىٰ عَن ذِكْرِنَا وَلَمْ يُرِدْ إِلَّا الْحَيَاةَ الدُّنْيَا

stopped even with an elephant."⁸⁰ The tricks of the lowly world vis-à-vis man's beliefs are even more dangerous, to the extent that man will not be able to do a thing. So avoid the problem from the start.

O wayfarers! Why is it that worldly people do not come to you for your companionship for a single day in wayfaring? If they come to you for a day, it is for some worldly benefit they wish to obtain. Your beliefs, methodology, goals, and lifestyle are in opposition to theirs. They are unwilling to be with you on the path, and it is for this reason that if you visit them, they say, "Here he goes again, talking about *taqwa*!"⁸¹ Can people of the path have relations with such individuals? You will slowly lose all of your spiritual gains.⁸²

---

80. Gulistan, Saadi Shirazi.

81. The word taqwa is a noun that comes from the root verb (و ق ي), meaning to protect something against that which may damage it. In the shari'ah, however, the word refers to protecting one's self from committing sins. Ayatullah Khushwaqt said, "The material and spiritual benefits of taqwa have been described in the Holy Qur'an when Allah (s) said, 'If the people of the towns had been faithful and Godwary, We would have opened for them blessings from the heaven and the earth.'" Mutahhari, p. 71, quoting the Holy Qur'an 7:96.

Ayatullah Jawadi Amuli, quoting the Holy Qur'an 65:2 said, "The believer with taqwa will never find himself forced into a corner in any task. This is because God has given him the power of discernment." Nobility in the Qur'an, Jawadi Amuli, p. 69.

82. "Leave alone those who take their religion for play and diversion and whom the life of this world has deceived." Holy Qur'an 6:70 وَذَرِ الَّذِينَ اتَّخَذُوا دِينَهُمْ لَعِبًا وَلَهْوًا وَغَرَّتْهُمُ الْحَيَاةُ الدُّنْيَا

Ayatullah Sa'adat Parwar said that interacting with worldly people is harmful. The harm is that they will not allow any of their capital to escape them, but they will destroy the capital of the wayfarer, which is his careful attention to Allah (s). Worldly people speak so much about work, earnings, and material benefits that the wayfarer will forget he was once on the path of spiritual wayfaring.

Exceptions to the Rule

Our teacher said to avoid interacting with worldly people "except to the extent that is necessary." What is the extent necessary? Necessity is not a positive thing. It means that man has a problem that has preoccupied him. For example, it is necessary for him to eat a bite of prohibited meat so that he does not die.[83] How much should he eat? If someone is about to die of thirst and there is only impure water, how much is permissible to drink? One pitcher? A few glasses? One glass? One spoonful? If by drinking a spoonful his thirst is abated and his life is spared, he should limit himself to that amount.[84] In times of necessity, man does not open his hands freely, rather he opens them to the extent necessary. A landlord once said to a respected man, "I do not want you staying here any longer, effective immediately." The respected man had nowhere to go, so he gathered his belongings into a corner of the room and occupied the least amount of space possible. That was the best he could do to minimize the harm. Similarly, interacting with worldly people should only be to the extent necessary.[85]

---

83. Here the following tradition of Imam Ali (a) is instructive: "The world for Allah's prophets and chosen servants is like a carcass from which it is not permissible to fill one's stomach except out of necessity." Rayshahri, V. 2, p. 892.

84. In accordance with the legal principle الضرورات تقدر بقدرها

85. Islam places heavy emphasis on the importance of maintaining relations with one's family, other believers, and society. Thus, in attempting

However, when it is said that interacting with worldly people—whose primary concerns are their food and entertainment—is harmful, this does not mean that one should offend or speak ill of them. Rather, interact with them in a pleasant and respectful manner. It is true that "To you your religion, and to me my religion,"[86] or put another way, they have their aims and we have ours, but one can withdraw from their company respectfully. What do we know? Perhaps one day they will gain interest in this path.

One who withdraws from worldly people, however, should never think he/she is better than them. If someone begins to feel this way, correct them by stating, "Who said you are better than anyone else?" Being better is related to one's end and final destination. Firstly, we do not know about the past deeds of others, but we do know about our own past sins. As for future acts, we have absolutely no knowledge. What do we know about the future misguidance we may be engulfed in?! What do we know about those worldly people? Perhaps they reach the highest of spiritual

---

to apply this etiquette to one's daily life, please refer to a qualified scholar for guidance to ensure one does not fall into extremes. [Translator]

According to Ayatullah Tahriri, avoiding heedless and sinful people is achieved in two ways: Firstly, through outward avoidance, which is necessary for those who are at the beginning of their spiritual journey; and secondly, through avoiding heedless people at the level of the heart. Islam does not approve of completely secluding oneself from people or of refraining from individual and social duties. See Tahriri, p. 367-8.

86. Holy Qur'an, 109:6 - لَكُمْ دِينُكُمْ وَلِيَ دِينِ

peaks! Therefore, the wayfarer—while not being inclined to worldly people—does not insult or belittle them [and always remembers the importance of maintaining relations with family and believers]. Nonetheless, "To you your religion, and to me my religion."[87]

---

87. "It must be born in mind that wayfaring and spiritual journey is not in contradiction with the wayfarer's existence in and interaction with the material world. The multiplicity in the external world always remains as it is, and the wayfarer finds unity within that multiplicity. A prominent gnostic once said, 'I lived among the people for thirty years. They thought that I was in their company and had constant association with them, whereas throughout this period I did not see or know anybody except God.'" Kernel of the Kernel, Tabataba'i, p. 23.

PART 3 - FOCUS

Etiquette 7
Concern Yourself with Yourself

"The wayfarer must focus his attention on himself and attend to himself. He should not spend his life talking about this-or-that person, even if not backbiting them, and should avoid useless speech."

Self-Vigilance (*Muraqabah*)[88]

Ayatullah Sa'adat Parwar advised us to focus our attention on ourselves. The etiquettes we are discussing explicitly or implicitly exist in the Holy Qur'an, which makes them the best of etiquettes. The Holy Qur'an states, "O you who believe! Take care of your own souls. He who strays cannot hurt you if you are guided."[89] This means to be attentive to yourself from every perspective, including

---

[88]. Muraqabah literally means to attentively watch and supervise something. Here, it refers to a state of self-vigilance, whereby the wayfarer ensures he does not neglect any of his duties. Ayatullah Sa'adat Parwar quotes his teacher Allamah Tabataba'i as having said, "Among the necessities of spiritual wayfaring is muraqabah from the beginning of the journey until its end." Thamarat al-Hayat, Sa'adat Parwar, V. 1, p. 32.

Allamah Tabataba'i also said, "One of the most important elements of and requirements in the path of wayfaring and spiritual journey is constant attention (muraqabah). From the first step that the traveler takes on the Path until the last step, he should never be negligent in observing muraqabah. This is one of the absolute necessities from the traveler. It should be known that muraqabah consists of various stages and levels. In the early phases of wayfaring, the traveler practices a different kind of muraqabah than at later stages. The higher the stages of levels one traverses and the more one advances toward perfection, the more intense and more profound one's muraqabah becomes—so much so that if it were to be imposed on a novice in the initial stages of wayfaring, he would not be able to bear it and would abandon wayfaring entirely; or he would be burnt out and consumed by it and perish… Through muraqabah the veils gradually turn thinner and eventually disappear…" Kernel of the Kernel, Tabataba'i, p. 19.

[89]. Holy Qur'an, 5:105 - يَا أَيُّهَا الَّذِينَ آمَنُوا عَلَيْكُمْ أَنفُسَكُمْ لَا يَضُرُّكُم مَّن ضَلَّ إِذَا اهْتَدَيْتُمْ إِلَى اللَّهِ مَرْجِعُكُمْ جَمِيعًا فَيُنَبِّئُكُم بِمَا كُنتُمْ تَعْمَلُونَ

matters related to your senses—such as eating, speaking, and looking—as well as less apparent matters related to one's heart and soul. Being attentive to ourselves does not require us to withdraw from others, rather, it requires that we be concerned with our own spiritual condition first and foremost.[90] This is accomplished by way of *muraqabah*.

Muraqabah requires that we be attentive to what we eat and drink, with whom we interact, what we say, etc.[91] For example, what do we eat? Do we eat halal or haram food? Was the food purchased with money acquired in a questionable manner? Do we overeat or do we eat an appropriate amount? Do we eat based on desire or necessity? Do we distribute and share with others what we ourselves eat? Why do we wear particular clothes? Is it to show off? Based on what criteria do we select the color, type, and mark of our clothing? Similarly, we must question ourselves about our interactions, conversations, and where we look.

---

90. Allah (s) introduces the Holy Messenger (s) as a role model for humanity (33:21). Prophet Muhammad (s) was the most attentive of all of mankind toward his own soul, yet his life is full of examples of selfless service to others and involvement in the social and political realms. Thus, giving priority and precedence to caring for one's own soul must be understood as an etiquette that encompasses our responsibilities towards others. It is a mistake to understand these concepts as being mutually exclusive. [Translator]

91. "If you have allowed your nafs to be free; have not performed self-accounting (muhasabah) and self-vigilance (muraqaba); and have been negligent—you have wasted your life and should fear a bad ending." Risaleh-e-Irfani, Sa'adat Parwar, p. 190.

This is self-vigilance. Ultimately, if our teacher did not mention any other etiquette, this one would encompass all the others and suffice. Focusing one's attention on oneself is not some imaginary statement. Start with the basic matters mentioned above and then give attention to all matters that will be counted among your actions.

There also exists within each of us desires, thoughts, negative opinions, and other inclinations that may push us toward sin. If these matters are not resolved, they may manifest themselves outwardly. For example, if from morning to evening our minds are occupied by negative or inappropriate thoughts, praying in congregation *(jama'ah)* will not have its intended effect. Praying in congregation is good, but with these negative thoughts, what can we accomplish?! These thoughts are us! Accepting and maintaining correct beliefs in relation to Allah (s), the Prophet (s), and the Imams (a); relying on Allah (s), and not holding pessimistic views in relation to Allah (s) – are important matters which make us who we are.

What do I think about Allah (s)? How present is He for me? How concerned is He with me? How much does He observe my actions, my thoughts, and what is in my heart? These beliefs are related to the self and being cautious about the self. I must be cautious that I am not distanced from Allah (s) so that I am not imprisoned by my ego. Some of the matters discussed in this section are important, and others are more important. It is important that I control my thoughts so I am not pursuing my desires, but to always see Allah's (s) presence is more important because if I accomplish that, the other matters will naturally follow.

Now, imagine if a man owns land but mistakenly builds his house on an adjacent lot belonging to another. When he is informed about his error, how will he feel? He will feel as though he does not own the house, since he built it on someone else's land. Ownership is connected to land, and owning a building is secondary to owning the land. This man spent his resources building, but now he feels like he wasted his wealth. Similarly, the concern man has for things other than his own spiritual state is like building a home on the land of another. One has wasted his most precious capital: time. Therefore, our spiritual teacher said the wayfarer's concern should be his own self.

Lessons from Your Body

Who is the "self" that we are being told to be cautious of? Is it our body? Before one can be cautious of his self, he must know who this self is. The Holy Prophet (s) said, "He who knows himself knows his Lord."[92] This self includes the body, so those who are able to correctly recognize their bodies will have the capacity to recognize Allah (s). Is it possible that man looks at and appreciates his fingertips with all their magnificence and then comes to a standstill on the path to perfection? Is it possible that one pays attention to the placement of each individual eyelash and still does not see Allah (s)? How many years do these eyelashes work for you? What can man produce that can last in this way?

Sometimes merchandise is valued because it is an antique and other times it is valued because it is new. Allah (s), however, has created something that maintains its value without being altered. This is an important matter, and if man pays attention to this, it is enough of a lesson. When man produces new and advanced merchandise, it means what came before is no longer suitable. However, Allah (s) has created eyelashes, eyes, eyebrows, noses, and lips that have remained from the time of Adam (a) until today, and there has never been a need to produce updated models. We live 60, 70 or 100 years and wonder, "How strange that

---

92. Bihar al-Anwar, V. 58, p. 99. مَنْ عَرَفَ نَفْسَهُ فَقَدْ عَرَفَ رَبَّهُ

these body parts have served us for so long!" In truth, these body parts have served mankind since the time of Adam (a)!

Another example is that of a car. At first it had a simple design, but today we see constant changes and advancements in the automotive industry. We say, "Look how much man has progressed!" but we should also say, "How little did we know that we did not build it this way from the start!" Allah (s) has created man's body in this very manner from the time of Adam (a) and has had no need to change or alter His creation. Allah (s) does not update the ear, rather it hears well and comprehends all types of sounds. Is it possible that one gives attention to such matters and does not see Allah (s)?

Our spiritual teacher advised all to pay attention to the miracle of the body, and see it like a teacher. and not state, "We did not have a teacher, and thus we did not understand the realities of life." Another example is this sneeze that we are unable to suppress despite all our power and free-will. Where did this high-speed sneeze come from? What is its function and benefit? Why do we sometimes sneeze a few times consecutively and other times just once? We have not given attention to such matters! At the most, when we sneeze, we say we have a cold and we take some medicine, whereas this very sneeze is a lesson in recognizing Allah (s). Also, pay attention to the various types of liquids that come from these bodies of ours. If someone wished to pay attention to and ponder over saliva, one or two years would not be sufficient. *Allahu Akbar!* One type of water comes from our nose, another from our eyes, and so on, each with its own composition and effects.

This body of ours has grandeur and complexity. Look at our fingernails. They have three sections: one that grows and becomes superfluous, which we trim; another in the middle of the nail; and a final section, which is a semi-circle. Research shows that one's health can be better understood by looking at this final section. For example, if one lacks this semi-circle, it is a sign of certain conditions. This is not a simple matter; it means that this last portion of our fingernail is connected to the rest of our body such that it can relay information about one's condition. This is a sign of the Creator's grandeur, which we acknowledge not simply so we can praise Him, but so He is known. Why don't we pay attention to ourselves?!

Ayatullah Sa'adat Parwar said to pay attention to yourself. Look at your hands and feet. Notice how the thumb joint only bends in one direction; if it bent in the other direction, what would happen? Pay attention to the length of our hands in proportion to the actions we perform with them, such as eating. If they were created a bit smaller or larger, what would occur? In a sense, our bodies and exteriors are also our own selves. These are not hidden matters that require a telescope or laboratory to observe; even the apparent is full of limitless signs. We could spend our lives paying attention to these matters, and while our lives would end, such wonders would not.

Allah (s) has made the entirety of creation a teacher for us—from the greatest of creations and prophets, our Master Muhammad (s), to common objects, to things that are apparently insignificant—all are our teachers, but we have abandoned taking lessons from them. If someone were to show us a machine that could perform multiple functions, we would say to ourselves, "What an astonishing machine! What an astonishing inventor!" We would be full of praise, whereas we have a body with astonishing internal and external capabilities, yet we give it no attention. What we have discussed thus far is the aspect of the self that is related to the body, but the body is not the whole self. The self that must be given our full attention is something more.

Establishing the Soul

If someone asks you who you are, what is your response? If we respond with our passport or bank account number, they will say, "But *who* are you?" If we state that our car is this or our house is that, they will say, "I did not ask what you own. Do not introduce yourself through what you own; introduce yourself by way of yourself." That is when we realize that we have not accomplished or obtained anything through which we can introduce ourselves. Unfortunately, we introduce ourselves by way of items or titles. Since our concern was never who we actually are, we are unable to leave impressions by way of our own selves. Rather, we allow other things to initiate our introductions. Our spiritual teacher said the wayfarer should not be this way: give attention to your own self.

Who is this self? When we say: my house, my car, my bank account, my phone, my computer, etc., all of these items are being given relation to the "my" or the "I" which signifies the self. Who is this "I"? If we were to consider the self as being confined to the body, then when we attribute ownership to ourselves by saying, for example, "my book", what we would really be saying is, "my body's book." This would be laughable, but perhaps some might accept it. To take it a step further, if we wanted to say "my body", would it then really mean "my body's body"? or if we stated, "My body is tired," are we really saying, "My body's body is tired"? If we define the self to simply be our body, many meaningless expressions begin to appear which are awkward and laughable because we are connecting terms and concepts that cannot be connected.

When we say I am going, what does this mean? My body is going? Or when we say I heard, I laughed, I read, I am sad, I am cheerful, or I am successful, what do we mean? We do not mean my body is successful; we mean I am successful. Here, I perceive something other than my body, which I perceive as successful. If I did not perceive it, then saying "I am successful" would be meaningless. Put another way, first I perceive whatever that "thing" is, then I perceive success. Therefore, that "me" or "self", which our spiritual teacher said the wayfarer must give attention to, is more than the body. That is because ascribing immaterial concepts to the body is meaningless. Something other than the body exists, which is primary, and that is what we connect these concepts to. It must have an immaterial capacity for such immaterial concepts to be connected to it.

This immaterial self is that which we perceive before the other aspects. For example, saying, "I perceive my hand," has no meaning unless we first perceive this "I." It is the self that is initially perceived, but since this perception occurs quickly, we do not give it attention. When we say, "I am going," the perception of this "I" is so instantaneous that we believe it is our body that is moving. When we say, "My hand is cut," we perceive the self so quickly that we do not even pause to consider it. Accordingly, in actions we initially perceive the self, but due to the speed of this perception, we are inattentive to it. This is unless man has trained himself to give attention to this matter. Therefore, an immaterial self exists and is perceived before any other matter.

When it is said, "He who knows himself knows his Lord,"[93] this is the immaterial self being referred to. In truth, by simply recognizing the existence of your immaterial self you recognize Allah (s). Likewise, we first perceive the self and then what is attributed or connected to it, but the matter is different when it comes to our relationship with Allah (s). The hadith does not state that whoever knows himself will come to know his Lord in the near future or in the distant future. There is no interval mentioned in this hadith. The relationship between knowing the "self" and knowing Allah (s) is one of equivalence, meaning if you know one, you immediately know the other. These concepts cannot be separated because it is impossible to know the self without first knowing Allah (s). We know ourselves through Allah (s), not the other way around.[94]

---

93. Ibid.
94. Ustadh Vazirifard expounded on this point by way of an example: Imagine a man standing in a house of mirrors. The man is the reality, and what exists in the mirrors are reflections or manifestations of the man. If the man recognized himself prior to entering the house of mirrors, he would recognize what he saw in the various mirrors as being reflections or manifestations of himself. If, however, the man did not recognize himself before entering, he would not be able to correctly recognize the reflections. Similarly, Allah (s) is the only reality, and a man who does not

This can be further explained when we see that Allah (s) has described the connection between Himself and man as follows: "And We are nearer to him than his jugular vein."[95] What is our jugular vein? It is not like the rest of our veins. If one or two other veins are cut, one can still survive, but the jugular vein is equivalent to life, meaning if it is cut, life is cut. When Allah (s) says He is closer to us than our jugular vein, it means He is closer to us than our own lives, as He is the Creator of life. The Creator must exist for the created to exist, so first He is, then we are.

If someone asks you if you are alive, will you delay your answer until you check your blood pressure or check for other signs of life? Of course not. Such signs are used by others who wish to determine whether we are alive, but if we ourselves want to know if we are alive, we immediately pay attention and witness that we are alive. We require no evidence as proof. Allah (s) is closer to us than our jugular vein, meaning He is closer to us than our own lives. From this angle, if we wish to perceive Allah (s), do we first perceive Him or ourselves as alive? Between two things, the one that is closer is perceived first. Since Allah (s) is closer to us than life itself, Allah's existence is immediately established.

---

recognize Allah (s) will be unable to correctly recognize or know himself, since he is a manifestation of Allah (s). [Translator]

95. Holy Qur'an, 50:16 - وَلَقَدْ خَلَقْنَا ٱلْإِنسَـٰنَ وَنَعْلَمُ مَا تُوَسْوِسُ بِهِ نَفْسُهُ وَنَحْنُ أَقْرَبُ إِلَيْهِ مِنْ حَبْلِ ٱلْوَرِيدِ

Allahu Akbar! In truth, the speed of this realization is such that it does not even require our attention. Put another way, life is such that without giving it attention, we know that we are alive, and if Allah is closer to us than our jugular veins, how much attention is really required to recognize Allah (s)? It is said that "Whoever knows himself knows his Lord," and we understand this close connection, but in truth, the one who gives attention to himself actually recognized Allah (s) first, and then recognized himself. It is "Through You, I have recognized You,"[96] and not that through myself I have recognized You. In truth we recognize Him and then ourselves through Him.[97]

---

96. Dua Abu Hamza al-Thumali, See Qummi, V. 1, p. 487.

97. "When we suppose two things, they would have an aspect they share and an aspect they differ in, each one would be composed of two aspects, but the Truth Almighty is One and Simple in essence and He does not have any composite nature (tarakkub) in any way. Therefore, it is impossible to know Him through something other than Him... In general, if one was to witness his Lord, he would know Him, and he would know his own self as well as everything else through Him. Thus, attentiveness in worship would be bestowed upon this person in this correct way. Without this witnessing, our attention towards Allah will only be a mental projection, whatever it may be." Risalat al-Wilayah, A Treatise on Islamic Mysticism and Spiritual Wayfaring, Muhammad Husayn Tabatabai, p. 70-72.

The Role of the Soul

The self that is so important is not just the body, but rather it is the immaterial soul that manages the body. For example, your body has eyes. If you wish to use your eyes to look, the soul manages that decision. In truth, this soul is the manager, master, and commander of the body, which—with all of its importance—is only the delegate and obedient servant of this master.

What are the wonders of that immaterial self, the soul? Are they inside or outside of our bodies? From where did these wonders enter our bodies and direct them? This self is so connected to us and our bodies that when the self intends something, the body immediately acts. This self has such an important role, and it commands and manages the body, but how much attention do we give to it? We all value our fingers, but that soul which moves these fingers, by simply intending to do so, is even more important.

Therefore, if one wishes to pay attention to himself, he must first understand who the self is, where it is, and how it entered his body. What is this connection between the soul and the body, that when it is severed, the body is incapable, and when it is strengthened, the body can act. Within which set of veins is this self located? None! But, where is it? Everywhere! It must be said that the relationship of the soul to the body is one of predominance. It is the soul that regulates, manages, controls, and rules the body. Thus, we must consider who this self is and where it came from? Is it another body inside our body that orders it around? Is it a pure, gasious substance that enters through our mouths and noses and has free will which enables the body to move?

Since the relationship between the soul and the body is one of predominance, the soul is more important than the body. When one's body parts sin, they are under the command of the self. When man does not want to sin, he does not need to physically restrain his body parts, as he possesses willpower which rules over his body and actions. Simply put, if man instructs each body part not to sin, they will not sin. If he tells his eyes not to sin, they will not sin. If he tells his tongue, "Do not speak badly; do not speak excessively; do not speak harshly; do not offend; do not lie; do not backbite; do not insult," etc. The tongue will not commit these actions and there will be no need for physical restraint. Although, some have placed a stone under their tongue to train themselves when it comes to their speech, even there, one's will-power is commanding one to speak or not. That stone under the tongue was only placed there as a reminder.

"So admonish, for you are only an admonisher, and are not there to compel them to believe."[98] Since man has free will, even the Prophet (s) served as a reminder for mankind and did not compel them. Man can choose

---

98. Holy Qur'an, 88:21-22 - فَذَكِّرْ إِنَّمَا أَنتَ مُذَكِّرٌ

to follow the Prophet (s) and to give priority to guidance over misguidance. Therefore, when our spiritual teacher said that the wayfarer must give attention to and focus on himself, he did not mean the body—although the body is also included—but the reality of the self, which is the soul.

Know the Soul to Transcend

Ayatullah Sa'adat Parwar wrote, "The wayfarer must be consumed with his own care." As we stated, the self is made up of a body and an immaterial soul, which controls this body and is primary. It is good for one to give attention to the physical body, not by giving in to its desires, but rather by paying close attention to it and pondering over it. But, one must give more attention to the primary aspect of the self—the soul—which is the controller, commander, and ruler of the body. It is said that knowing Allah (s) is not that one sits in the corner of one's home in spiritual retreat until finding Allah (s). Allah (s) is everywhere, and He is closer to us than we are to ourselves. If we desire to truly recognize Allah (s), we cannot do so without giving Him our attention. It is He who enables us to recognize Him, and this is only understood when man correctly understands himself.

Our teacher's writing, "The wayfarer must be consumed with his own care," is not from the perspective that one is occupied only with oneself and remains at this stage of understanding. Rather, it is so that one understands himself in order to transcend himself and reach a level where he sees that Allah (s) is the true existent. Reaching such a station is only accomplished by way of careful attention to where this self came from. Did it always exist, or did someone bring it into existence? If it existed by itself, then we should have had pre-eternal awareness, and not awareness of 50, 60, or 70 years. Since we lack this pre-eternal awareness, we inherently recognize that this body and self were brought into being by another. Therefore, we must transcend this self and reach the One that brought about this self. It is from this perspective that it was said to be consumed with one's own care.

Obstacles to Self-Refinement: Fault-Finding

Whatever we occupy ourselves with, other than self-refinement, diverts our attention from self-refinement. This is true even if we wish for it not to be the case. A matter that often distracts one from self-refinement is inspecting the actions of others and finding fault in them. This occurs through our speaking and acting in ways that are not our responsibility, and such conduct results in us moving away from the pull of self-refinement.

If one enters a magnetic field, he is pulled toward the magnet. At the same time, the magnetic field of every magnet has a limit, and if one exits the field, they are no longer attracted to the magnet. For example, when a nail enters a magnetic field, the magnet pulls it in, but if the nail reaches a certain point outside the reach of the magnetic field, it can no longer be pulled in.

The magnet is Allah (s) and the magnetic field is our attention to Him (s). That which pulls us in the direction of Allah (s) is our attention to Allah (s). Allah (s) is giving us attention and is close to us, but we can be either close to, or far from Allah (s). When we do not give Him our attention, we move away from Him and eventually get to a point where He no longer pulls us in. However, as we increase our attention towards Allah (s), our recognition of Allah (s) increases accordingly.

Obstacles to Self-Refinement: Speaking Excessively

If one gives more attention to the self, the result will be an increase in his attention towards Allah (s). Among the actions that lessen our attention to Allah (s) is speaking excessively, and this is especially true when we speak about other people or about useless matters. Sometimes one is constantly occupied with the shortcomings of so-and-so; how tall or short so-and-so is; how fat or skinny so-and-so is; or how rich or poor so-and-so is. Assuming such speech is not backbiting, it still takes our attention away from Allah (s). If such speech is backbiting or slander, however, then not only will it decrease our attention towards Allah (s), but it will also be classified as a sin, resulting in our becoming distant from Allah (s).

When one becomes distant from Allah (s), he becomes distant from himself. "And do not be like those who forget Allah, so He makes them forget their own souls."[99] If you become distant from Allah (s), He also becomes distant from you and will lessen His attention towards you, as you have left the magnetic field of His attention. Giving attention to Allah (s) is within our capacity, and only our forgetfulness and negligence stand as obstacles. Thus, we become distant because of our own actions and then forget our own souls.

---

99. Holy Qur'an, 59:19 - وَلَا تَكُونُوا كَٱلَّذِينَ نَسُوا ٱللَّهَ فَأَنسَىٰهُمْ أَنفُسَهُمْ أُوْلَٰٓئِكَ هُمُ ٱلْفَٰسِقُونَ

"And do not be like those who forget Allah, so He makes them forget their own souls."[100] When we forget our souls, we also forget Allah (s). That is the nature of this connection. In the verse we see that forgetting Allah (s) is equivalent to forgetting our own souls. It is said that one who is occupied with himself forgets the shortcomings of others. This is because the soul, which has both positive and negative attributes, is both potentially sinful or God-conscious, and is so vast that if man wishes to be occupied by it, he cannot be occupied by anything else.

The Holy Prophet (s) said, "Blessed is the man who is so occupied with his own defects that he does not notice the defects of other people."[101] If man is busy with his own shortcomings, he will not have any opportunity to be concerned with the shortcomings of others. But, one must honestly be so concerned with his own faults that he drowns in the ocean of his shortcomings and does not have the opportunity to concern himself with the faults of others. From this perspective, our teacher has said to stay occupied

---

100. Ibid.
101. In relation to this tradition, Imam Khomeini said, "How ugly it is for a man with thousands of defects to neglect his own and attend to those of others, thereby adding them to the heap of his own defects! Were man to explore his own states, conduct, and acts—devoting himself to their correction—his affairs would be reformed. But, for him to regard himself as free of defect is the height of his ignorance. For no defect is worse than this, that man should be unaware and negligent of his own defects, yet be attentive to the defects of others, while he himself is a mass of defects and shortcomings." Forty Hadith, Khomeini, Hadith 19, p. 328.

with your own improvement and not to speak about others, even if you are not backbiting or insulting them.

Occupying yourself with the affairs and shortcomings of others, no matter to what degree, is harmful. The friends of Allah *(Awliya)* consider this to be a bad trait. For example, if someone says that so-and-so is in a good financial condition, to the same extent that he has given unnecessary attention to another, he has been negligent of himself. This is because the financial condition of another person has nothing to do with us for us to speak about it. However, if there was some relevance to this statement, such as wanting to suggest borrowing from so-and-so to give to so-and-so, then there is no problem in it. Otherwise, what need was there for such a remark?

Thus, try to avoid such statements, and do not justify such conduct by stating, "It was not backbiting or slander!" That is being negligent towards the self by being occupied with others. We said that we should be so occupied with our own reformation that we do not focus on others, but we have done the opposite. Avoid discussions, actions, and statements that have nothing to do with us, and instead focus on ourselves. If man was occupied with his own self, he would have discovered his shortcomings and addressed them. When one knows himself, he enters the vast ocean of *Tawhid*. If the *Awliya* limit their socializations or must be prodded to speak, it is because they know that every word and action is being accounted for. They are not unfriendly.

Rather, they are cheerful, friendly, and educated, but they are silent because there is a subject that is more important to them than their own words: controlling their lowly desires. Therefore, they have drowned themselves in vigilant care.

Our spiritual teacher said, "The wayfarer must be occupied with himself." This is a vast topic and includes some other points to give attention to. One matter is that the wayfarer should be one who is careful and engages in self-vigilance *(Muraqabah)* and self-accounting *(Muhasabah)*.[102] He should know the reason for his actions, words, and glances. He should know for whom he is performing these actions. Is there a benefit in it for his own soul, or is his attention on others?

---

102. Muhasabah is the process by which a wayfarer takes account of his actions daily to ensure he is performing his duties in accordance with his stage of wayfaring. According to Imam al-Kadhim (a), "He who does not take account of his soul each day is not from among us." al-Kafi, al-Kulayni, V. 2, p. 453.

Imam Ali (a) has said, "Appoint a watcher over yourself from within yourself." Al-Amudi Ghurar al-Hikam, narration 2429.

Ayatullah Sa'adat Parwar said, "Muhasabah and Muraqabah are mandatory in relation to all of your actions and statements, and not just once a year or once a month, but rather at least daily, although Muhasabah every hour and Muraqabah every moment is what is preferred." Pand Nameh-e-Sa'adat, Sa'adat Parwar, p. 34.

He added, "Whoever wishes to be among the Ahl al-Akhirah must correct his speech and action by way of constant self-accounting and self-vigilance…" Sirr al-Isra, Sa'adat Parwar, p. 181.

The wayfarer should be in heaven at this very moment, meaning the particulars of his actions should be heavenly because it is these very actions that become his heaven. In heaven, there is neither frivolous talk nor sin: "Wherein they will not hear any vain talk."[103] Therefore, one should be the same here in order to create such a heaven. Every gathering of ours should emit the fragrance of heaven. In this way, even if we lack positive heavenly characteristics, we can at least avoid negative characteristics and bring about a heavenly environment. If our speech does not include backbiting, insults, frivolousness, speaking about others, etc., then it has the color and smell of heaven, as the Qur'an states: "wherein there will be neither any vain talk nor sinful speech."[104]

Ayatullah Sa'adat Parwar said to avoid useless speech. Society considers the loss of wealth to be a significant loss, but in truth, if man loses his money, he has not lost a thing. Rather, loss is when one forgets himself and gives attention to all else: "Say, 'Indeed the losers are those who ruin themselves…'"[105] Put another way, other than this loss, no other loss exists. The Qur'an does not state that one who loses his wealth, position, and status is a loser. Rather, the Qur'an states the loser is he who does not give attention to himself.

---

103. Holy Qur'an, 88:11 - لاَّ تَسْمَعُ فِيهَا لَٰغِيَةً
104. Holy Qur'an, 52:23 - يَتَنَازَعُونَ فِيهَا كَأْسًا لَّا لَغْوٌ فِيهَا وَلَا تَأْثِيمٌ
105. Holy Qur'an, 39:15 - فَاعْبُدُوا مَا شِئْتُم مِّن دُونِهِ ۗ قُلْ إِنَّ الْخَاسِرِينَ الَّذِينَ خَسِرُوا أَنفُسَهُمْ وَأَهْلِيهِمْ يَوْمَ الْقِيَامَةِ ۗ أَلَا ذَٰلِكَ هُوَ الْخُسْرَانُ الْمُبِينُ

7 - CONCERN YOURSELF WITH YOURSELF

Etiquette 8
Make Silence Your Motto

"Make silence your motto, except when needed, because most slips are caused by the tongue."

Controlling the Tongue

Man uses his tongue to taste food, eat, swallow, and speak, as we discussed in Etiquette 7. Good emanates from a tongue that is under control. For example, without the tongue we would be unable to be guided by the speech of the Prophets (a). But, if the tongue is not used to speak appropriately, it is dangerous. Thus, silence and holding back our tongue is usually better than speaking.

Silence is a good thing. When one speaks he must be careful not to be talkative because being talkative results in one falling into mistakes and errors. "One who increases his speech, increases his errors."[106] Therefore, what reason does man have to continuously speak? Allah (s) has given man a tongue so he can speak at the appropriate time. When man speaks about his beliefs, advises others, guides someone away from danger, says something that brings about happiness, such speech is good. However, your typical speech—even that which does not include backbiting, insults, lies, etc.—often reaches a sensitive and dangerous point. We see that many family disagreements begin with speech, and gradually reaches a more sensitive and dangerous place. Accordingly, the tongue has an important role in preserving or destroying the family environment.

It is said that each morning when man wakes up, his body parts speak to the tongue, stating, "By Allah (s),

---

106. من كثر كلامه كثر خطاءه Majlisi, V. 68, p. 286.

leave us alone today. Do not throw us into the fire of hell!" The tongue opens the doors of hell for other body parts. In contrast, one's shortcomings are hidden by one's silence. Those who have no good qualities should at the very least allow their bad qualities to remain hidden. As long as one has not opened his mouth, his character is not known.[107]

One rarely accumulates sins while being silent. Instead, opportunities for thought and contemplation come about. If we are silent, the opportunity for contemplation about the world of existence, our own position in that world, the creation of the universe, the mercy of Allah (s), and other such matters come about. Unfortunately, we run from silence. We say to the one who is silent, "Why are you so quiet?" as if the default position is that everyone should talk even if there is nothing to talk about. Who said the default position should be talking? We have confused the default position with the exception. The default position is silence.

Do not take issue with someone who is silent. It is good for man to be silent and wise rather than talkative and ignorant. Fear of silence, avoidance of silence, and unacquaintance with silence result in one lacking depth. We fear silence and contemplation. We are not ready to be silent even for ten minutes! Allah (s) has invited us to think and contemplate, and this requires silence. But, since we

---

107. اللسان ميزان الانسان "The tongue is the scale for examining man." Al-Amudi, Ghurar al-Hukam, narration 1282.

have changed our default to speech, we avoid silence and contemplation.

For example, some may fear darkness, but physical darkness can have benefits, as it takes man's attention away from material concerns and prepares the grounds for contemplation and thought. We have changed our default position. Rather than silence being our motto, speaking is our motto.[108] When the opportunity for silence comes about, we are constantly talking. Be a bit more silent. We have spent long hours speaking at times when silence was more beneficial.

It is possible that some are more talkative than others.[109] Be careful, though, as being talkative can bring about many problems. Sometimes one statement that should not have been said brings about tremendous difficulty, just as one match can ignite a fire that brings down thousands of trees.[110]

---

108. It is narrated in Misbah al-Shariyah that Imam Sadiq (a) said, "Silence is the motto of the lovers of God, and in it lies the Lord's pleasure. It is the virtue of the Prophets (s) and the motto of the pure ones." Also see Majlisi, v.15, p.186.

109. It is said that souls are not identical to one another and some of them incline to certain noble characteristics more so than others. Thus, acquiring certain traits of the soul may be easier for some than others. [Translator]

110. "Being talkative…is a characteristic of worldly people. The reason for this is that in all conditions, man is either self-vigilant about matters related to the next world or is attending to worldly matters, and being self-vigilant about matters related to the next world is not possible while

Our motto must be silence.[111] A motto or slogan means a statement that we give precedence to in our actions. For example, if our slogan is independence, then certain actions logically follow. We would ensure we are economically independent. We would ensure we are politically independent, meaning we would not look to global hegemony for direction when making decisions. Regarding cultural independence, we should not rely on the books or syllabi of others in our educational programming. A slogan of independence is meaningless if we act otherwise.

Therefore, we should change our motto to silence.[112] The specifications of a motto are: firstly, that we believe in it, that people know us by it, and that it is not something we change daily; and secondly, a motto should hold some weight. If we select silence as our motto, we should take the necessary steps and efforts for its establishment. This requires perseverance. Allah (s) likes that we reflect His characteristics. He is the determined one, and the owner of determination. Accordingly, His slave should also be determined or should at least be on the path to becoming so.

One of the areas in which man can easily align himself with the will of Allah (s) and become determined

---

being talkative." Sirr al-Isra, Sa'adat Parwar, V. 1, p. 77.
111. See Footnote 108.
112. Consult a qualified spiritual teacher prior to implementing this etiquette so as not to fall into extremes. [Translator]

is in the matter of silence. Remaining silent is easier than any other action. It has no costs and requires no literacy or knowledge of logic, Arabic grammar, or any other subject. As tired as man gets from speaking, which requires energy, he does not get tired from silence. However, we have made the easiest action into the most difficult one by confusing our default positions. We are headed in the wrong direction and must return to the correct path. It is for these very reasons we do not reach perfection. Therefore, we must give attention to silence and make it our motto.

Do not consider silence to be difficult, as it is the easiest of actions to perform.[113] One who considers easy matters to be difficult will fail when faced with difficult matters. All of those who reached spiritual perfection were people of silence. The poem, "Five things make the incomplete ones of this world complete; Silence, and hunger, and night-vigil, solitude, and steady remembrance keep,"[114] has been a protocol of the wayfarers. Their first action is *samt*, which is defined as silence accompanied by reflection.[115] A wise silence stemming from concentration.

---

113. "al-Rabi ibn Khuthaym used to have a paper on which he would write every word that he uttered during the day. Then he would take account of himself at night to see if what he had said was to his advantage or disadvantage." Treatise attributed to Bahr al-Uloom, p. 230.

114. This line of poetry is often attributed to Sayyid Muhammad Jawad Sadr Amuli. Another variation is attributed to Shah Qasim Anwar. See Treatise attributed to Bahr al-Uloom, p. 233.

115. "Silence (samt) is defined as controlling one's tongue from that which is not necessary and being satisfied with the least amount of speech

It is not that one is unable to speak coherently or lacks competency. Rather, one is competent and knows how to speak well, but chooses not to.

When some of our great scholars gathered with one another, their sessions passed in mostly silence rather than speech. And, if such sessions included speech, such speech deserved to be seized and benefited from. However, most of these sessions passed in silence. For some scholars, the default condition of their gatherings was silence. When one's external speech decreases, their inner speech gains expressiveness. In this manner, people can sit across from one another in silence while speaking to one another with the language of their hearts. We who sit and observe such individuals think nothing has occurred and nothing was said, but an hour later when the parties depart from one another, it is as if they have spoken about all of existence. When our tongues are busy speaking there is no possibility for the tongues of our hearts to open. May Allah (s) allow us to become accustomed to silence so that at the very least we avoid the fright of hell.[116]

---

that is necessary." Treatise attributed to Bahr Al-Uloom, p. 173.

116. Imam Baqir (a) said, "Truly our followers are the mute ones." al-Kafi, V. 2, p. 113. قَالَ سَمِعْتُ أَبَا جَعْفَرٍ ع يَقُولُ إِنَّمَا شِيعَتُنَا الْخُرْسُ.

8 - MAKE SILENCE YOUR MOTO   127

Etiquette 9
Avoid Your Desires

"Avoid selfish desires as much as possible and with discretion. In any matter in which [the nafs is overly inclined], perform an istikharah so that there is at least a justification for the act."

Righteous Actions

It is not far-fetched to say that the most fundamental element of spiritual wayfaring is opposing one's desires. One should reach a stage wherein he has annihilated himself in Allah (s). In reality, he sees Allah (s) ruling over all things, and his desires have no authority. If man performs an action that is apparently good, gnostic, revolutionary, spiritual, in obedience to Allah (s), but the action is tainted by the ego, this action will not benefit him. It is possible that others may benefit from the action, but there is no benefit for the actor in this scenario because he has not been self-vigilant with regard to his desires. Such actions are not considered good deeds, as righteous deeds do not include selfishness or ego.[117] Such deeds are not considered *Tawhidi* and do not raise one's rank. It is *Tawhidi* actions that raise the call of *Tawhid*—"and He elevates righteous conduct"[118]—while actions tainted by ego are too weak to do so.

It is said, "To Him ascends the good word."[119] The "good word" is the first *shahadah*, which equates to *Tawhid*. When man becomes a monotheist he directs all of his work for the sake of Allah (s). "To Him ascends the good word, and He elevates righteous conduct..."[120] Therefore, when

---

117. "In relation to acts of worship, give attention to the quality of an action and not the quantity." Resaleh-e-Irfani, Sa'adat Parwar, p. 186.
118. Holy Qur'an, 35:10 - جَمِيعًا إِلَيْهِ يَصْعَدُ ٱلْكَلِمُ ٱلطَّيِّبُ وَٱلْعَمَلُ ٱلصَّـٰلِحُ يَرْفَعُهُ
119. Ibid.
120. Ibid.

the ego is not present, righteous actions constantly raise one's level of *Tawhidi* understanding and one's *ma'rifah* of Allah (s).

"Whoever acts righteously, it is for his own soul…"[121] Whoever performs a righteous action will himself benefit, and this effect apparently appears on his very being. If that action is not righteous or good it is not performed for the self. Rather, one has acted against his own interest. "…and whoever does evil, it is to [the soul's] detriment…"[122] As such, if someone performs a bad action he has harmed himself.

The fundamental principle in spiritual wayfaring is that man should not give attention to his lower self. This means acting in a manner that removes ego, arrogance, selfishness, and self-worship from one's thoughts, actions, words, glances, and silence—and the sooner the better. If man wishes to lessen the shade of his ego, he should not give the self an opportunity to rule over the soul by acting on whatever it desires. Rather, as much as possible he should lessen his ego's desires and refrain from acting on them because acting on one's lower desires is equivalent to accepting the rule of the self. If man selects himself as a leader and guide, we know this will lead to a bad ending, and it is from this perspective that our spiritual teacher said

---

121. Holy Qur'an, 41:46 - مَّنْ عَمِلَ صَالِحًا فَلِنَفْسِهِ وَمَنْ أَسَاءَ فَعَلَيْهَا وَمَا رَبُّكَ بِظَلَّامٍ لِّلْعَبِيدِ
122. Ibid.

to avoid your desires as much as possible.[123]

Avoiding one's desires does not mean man avoids actions necessary for his life and progress. Rather, those matters which are only related to the gratification of the senses should be avoided. Lower desires are those desires that one enjoys but have no other benefit. Our spiritual teacher said to deny the self such apparent pleasures. This does not mean one avoids an action just because one desires it. If man's desire is in line with Allah's (s) divine will, there is no problem in one performing such actions. For example, you either prefer praying at home or at the mosque. If you prefer praying at the mosque, this conforms with Allah's (s) command and the *shariah*. If you prefer praying at home without an excuse, however, this is an unsubstantiated desire that should be avoided.

As much as you give in to and foster your lower desires, the hostility of these desires toward your soul increases. This is contrary to some external enemies whose enmity towards you may decrease if you show affection. Notably, however, some of the powerful countries in the world today are not like this and instead take advantage of your affection. One must firmly stand in opposition to

---

123. Ayatullah Sa'adat Parwar quotes Ayatullah Bahjat as having said, "Avoiding one's desires is not an easy matter. Rather, it is very difficult. However, if this station is obtained in a gradual manner one will reach a point where one's nafs will be under your control." Risaleh-e-Irfani, Sa'adat Parwar, p. 185.

such arrogant powers. "Repel ill conduct with that which is best."[124] This command does not apply to one's own soul because the more attention you give it, the more it will desire. If today one desires a bite of *haram* food and accommodates that desire, tomorrow the *nafs* will desire another *haram* item and another the day after. If the *nafs* takes one step forward it will cast you ten steps back. Therefore, as our spiritual teacher said, avoid your desires.

---

124. Holy Qur'an, 23:96 - اِدْفَعْ بِٱلَّتِى هِىَ أَحْسَنُ ٱلسَّيِّئَةَ نَحْنُ أَعْلَمُ بِمَا يَصِفُونَ

Seeking What Is Khayr *(Istikharah)*

Ayatullah Sa'adat Parwar added that if one was deciding between two equivalent actions–meaning that the performance of one or the other would make no real difference– he should seek what is *khayr* from Allah (s) by way of an *Istikharah*.[125] This way, he would have a reason to select one action over the other. Similarly, if there is no difference in the performance of either action, our teacher said to perform the action one prefers least in order to train the soul. Growth is in opposing desires. Here, opposing one's desires is not in order to obtain any external result, but rather to train and nurture one's soul. This strengthens one in spiritual wayfaring on the path to perfection because ultimately man must reach a stage where he sees his own desires as irrelevant.

To reach the stage wherein one does not see himself, one must begin with simple matters, meaning one should oppose his desires in apparently insignificant matters which will result in one not seeing their own will and self. Man cannot become a champion high-jumper overnight, for example. He must practice for years, beginning with small

---

125. Lexically, Istikharah means to seek khayr, or goodness. As an Islamic term it refers to seeking goodness or guidance from Allah (s) in selecting the best path forward in a particular matter. Istikharah is commonly performed with either prayer beads or the Holy Qur'an. Our scholars suggest that it is appropriate to perform an Istikharah when one has exercised his intellect and consulted with others, but remains in a state of perplexity in choosing between two seemingly good options. [Translator]

steps. To think he can suddenly jump two or three meters high is delusional. Only through effort and starting with reasonable goals will man reach a higher goal. Opposing one's carnal self is much more difficult than the high-jump and therefore requires longer practice and more prerequisites.

An *Istikharah* should not be performed for trivial matters. The priority must be to act in accordance with Islamic law and our intellects. When there is a matter about which Islamic law is silent, Allah (s) has given us an intellect and we must use it accordingly. Therefore, that one performs an *Istikharah* for every action will make one weak-willed and intellectually incapable. See what the intellect suggests [and consult with others]. If a time comes when the intellect does not have the capacity to select the best route and one remains confused, [only then] perform an *Istikharah* intending to act on Allah's (s) will, not your own.

Avoiding Desires, with Discretion

Ayatullah Sa'adat Parwar stated that as much as to one's capacity and with discretion, avoid your desires. Some say that opposing our desires is not our responsibility because it is not practical for us, but when our teacher said "to one's capacity," he meant that there are times when man is able to oppose his desires and times when he is not. If he opposes his desires in the latter cases, it may lead to harm or upset others, which is disliked in the *shariah*.

For example, a fasting person may prefer to pray *Salat ul-Maghrib* before dinner, which is also preferable according to the *shariah*. But one's family or guests prefer to eat together before praying. Here, if one prays first, he will upset others. Thus, he should first eat, and Allah (s), who is *al-Jabbar* (the All-Powerful), will compensate the wayfarer. Since he was unable to oppose his desires as he wished by praying before eating, Allah (s) will place the good effects of opposing his desires and praying at the earliest time in his action of eating with his family or guests. Thus, our teacher stated, "to one's capacity," meaning that man should use his discretion in accordance with the intellect and shariah. If in one's discretion it is not appropriate to oppose one's permissible desires in a particular situation, he has no duty to do so.

PART 4 – FREEDOM

Etiquette 10
Deliberation and Consultation

"Do not get involved in any work or endeavor without deliberation, even if this takes a long time. In this regard, consulting with your spiritual teacher and fellow wayfarers is very necessary."

Deliberation

A wayfarer should enter every task with deliberation and forethought. He should not immediately proceed with whatever task someone suggests, whatever action that comes to mind, or with whatever opportunity that comes about. This includes in relation to selecting a teacher, which is one of the best actions. Whenever someone would go to our spiritual teacher Ayatullah Sa'adat Parwar to ask for guidance in wayfaring, the Ayatullah would not immediately accept them as a student. Instead, he would say, "Go and ponder over this matter of spiritual wayfaring. Think about whether you can take on this responsibility. Do you have the patience and capacity? Ask people about me." Our teacher would keep them waiting so they had the opportunity to ponder and think deeply over their decision in selecting a teacher. It is not appropriate for a teacher to immediately provide protocols and specific instructions, which is an unfortunate trend these days. One must be given time to ponder whether he will be successful on this path. Do not get involved in any matter without deliberation.[126]

In relation to pondering over whether to begin spiritual wayfaring or not, some say, "Our life has passed us

---

126. قَالَ سَمِعْتُ أَبَا عَبْدِ اللَّهِ ع يَقُولُ الْعَامِلُ عَلَىٰ غَيْرِ بَصِيرَةٍ كَالسَّائِرِ عَلَىٰ غَيْرِ الطَّرِيقِ لاَ يَزِيدُهُ سُرْعَةُ السَّيْرِ إِلَّا بُعْداً.
Imam Sadiq (a) said, "One who acts without insight is like one who travels without a (clear) path: the faster his speed, the further he gets from his goal." al-Kafi, V. 1, p. 43.

by! We do not have time to sit and ponder and deliberate anymore!" In response we say, "Even if 40 years have passed and you have not begun wayfaring, no problem. Add another six months and think about it some more." If one begins wayfaring and fails, it is potentially harmful and their spiritual condition will worsen. Conversely, if one ponders, deliberates, and takes a correct path, he can make up for his past mistakes.

Consultation

Ayatullah Sa'adat Parwar said, "Consulting with your spiritual teacher and fellow wayfarers is very necessary."[127] Consultation with one's spiritual teacher is good and necessary in matters related to spiritual wayfaring. Some consult their teacher about matters such as whether they should buy something, get their car fixed, etc. They suppose their teacher is familiar with the stock market and will provide them information from the unseen realms. When it is said to consult your spiritual teacher, it means in matters related to spiritual wayfaring.

Note that consulting friends does not mean obtaining protocols and special instructions from them. Sometimes fellow wayfarers sit together and discuss matters that they may have heard. For example, someone received a particular *dhikr* or performed a certain act of worship. Thereafter, someone else may act on what was discussed thinking they have consulted fellow wayfarers. Such conduct is ineffective.

Being scattered and disorganized is an obstacle to gaining proximity to Allah (s). If man purifies his intention and takes serious action, his affairs will be put in order. If a wayfarer instead acts on one instruction from last night's discussion with friends and then on another instruction

---

127. Imam Ali (a) said, "The one who suffices himself with his own opinion endangers himself." Nahjul Balagha, Saying 211.

from social media, such scattered actions do nothing more than create a collection of scattered thoughts and ideas. Thereafter, when one does not reach one's intended result, he says, "Why am I like this?! Why is it that I did everything, but I was still not fixed?" In truth, the problem is just that: he did everything! Must man perform every act of canonical worship? Some are occupied with uncommon recommended acts, long invocations, attending this or that gathering, and such [heavy duties] may cause stress. Allah (s) did not make these matters obligatory for a reason. The wayfarer must deliberate about his methodology and actions, as only that will bring about benefit.

Consult with others to identify the appropriate path. Deliberation, pondering, and consultation exist so when one slips, he is not occupied by scattered thoughts or divided attention which keeps the wayfarer distant from the path. This is extremely important. Note that if another person obtains a spiritual instruction from a teacher, that does not mean the same instruction is good for you. If one gets a prescription from a doctor, does that automatically mean the doctor would prescribe the same to you? This is not the case. Rather, he may write you a prescription for a different medicine or for the same medicine but with a different dosage. Accordingly, it is not the case that every spiritual instruction we obtain from any source will be beneficial for us. Therefore, deliberate and seek consultation in all matters.

Etiquette 11
Mysteries of the Path

"Do not share the spiritual matters that one encounters with anyone except for the spiritual teacher, until the wayfarer reaches the stage of certainty (Itminan)."

Guarding the Mysteries of the Path

Certain spiritual states may come about for a wayfarer.[128] Since these states are pleasant, one may wish to share what he has experienced with others. However, since the *nafs* enjoys sharing such experiences, doing so is akin to following one's desires and will ruin the wayfarer's spiritual state. Furthermore, if one shares his experience with others, they may respond with statements that may distract or misguide the wayfarer. Therefore, there is no reason for one to share his spiritual states with others. If the wayfarer shares these matters with his teacher, it is because his teacher knows the spiritual condition of his student. Some speak about their teachers as if they have a detailed and encompassing knowledge of their students' spiritual conditions…and perhaps they do.

If someone visits a specialized doctor for ten years, that doctor will know the patient's conditions and will be best qualified to treat the patient. When it comes to spiritual wayfaring the matter is much the same. We will not exaggerate this matter as some do, but at the very least, one's teacher is best qualified to treat one's spiritual

---

128. For example, Allamah Tabataba'i narrates his first vision being a conversation he had with Prophet Idris (a). Allamah added, "One should not undertake ascetic practices to strengthen and/or display special mental and psychic power in any way and form, because such a person no longer worships God…on the contrary, it is his own soul that he worships…" See Kernel of the Kernel, Tabataba'i, p. 36 & 72.

ailments. Therefore, share matters of spiritual wayfaring that come about only with one's teacher.

The one who shares his spiritual states with others and then with his teacher is like the one who shares the details of his sickness with 10 doctors and obtains 10 different prescriptions and medications: he will ultimately need a specialist after seeing no results. This is not a correct course of action. If the wayfarer has really accepted that his teacher is a specialist in matters pertaining to spiritual wayfaring, he should have no need to share his spiritual states, dreams, and visions with this or that person. If what was seen or experienced is inconsequential, keep it to yourself, and if it was of substance and is relevant to spiritual wayfaring, only share it with your teacher.

Our spiritual teacher said that this should continue until one reaches the station of certainty *(Itminan)*.[129] One who reaches this station will not be easily disturbed or influenced by the remarks of others. If a wayfarer shares certain experiences with others, they may respond in a manner that flatters, disturbs, or distresses the wayfarer. However, if one reaches *Itminan*, wherein he will not be affected by anyone's remarks, there is no problem sharing

---

129. The author states that this station is reached when one is completely satisfied with Allah's (s) decree. See Holy Qur'an, 89:27-28.

these experiences to the extent that is necessary.[130]

But, it should not be that one tells everything to everyone, as revealing such matters is in opposition to the custom of the path. On this path, the more one's mouth is closed and locked, the better. In this regard, anyone other than one's teacher should be treated as a stranger. It is said to avoid strangers, but it should be known that "strangers" is a gradational term. Even if one has friends who are spiritual wayfarers, those friends are considered strangers compared to one's spiritual teacher. Therefore, it is better that the wayfarer does not share these matters with others even if the wayfarer has reached *Itminan*. Preserve matters that are between you and Allah (s). Do we share what is in our most precious jewelry box with everyone? Thieves are potentially everywhere. Therefore, our default position should be silence on these matters.

A question that may arise here is, "Why does a wayfarer still need to mention such matters to his teacher after he reaches *Itminan*?" In response, it can be said that

---

130. It should be noted that even the trustworthy stories related about the experiences of the great Urafa, such as Allamah Sayyid Ali Qadi, Allamah Tabataba'i, Ayatullah Bahjat, Allamah Hasanzadeh Amuli, are only a small sampling of the realities these souls encountered. Such stories are related to the general public to guide or strengthen their faith. [Translator] For example, Ayatuallah Sa'adat Parwar mentions that he shares some matters, "to show how the Divine Hand trained me from my childhood until the demise of the of the later teacher [Allamah Tabataba'i], and so that it serves as an eye-opener for those to come." Tahriri, p. 78.

even if a wayfarer reaches this station, his teacher has reached a higher position among the Stations of Certainty. It is therefore still necessary for a wayfarer to share his condition and benefit from his teacher.

Etiquette 12
A Positive Outlook

"Avoid thinking negatively of Allah's servants. Instead, one should think of reforming one's self and becoming so introspective that the shortcomings of others become invisible to him. Note, however, that the obligation to enjoin good (al-amru bi al-ma'ruf) and forbid evil (al-nahyu an al-munkar) is another matter."

Abstain from Holding Negative Opinions About Others

Here when Allah's servants are mentioned, it could mean all of mankind generally, or Allah's (s) choice servants in particular. In any case, we do not accurately recognize others, and we only see the exterior and apparent condition of a person and their actions. Some people may not impress us apparently, but their esoteric reality is that of a pure heart. From this perspective, when we see individuals who apparently are not of a high spiritual stature, we must say to ourselves, "Perhaps this individual has a pure heart and is 10-times better than me!" Rather than suspecting or holding pessimistic opinions about others, we should hold these negative opinions about ourselves.[131] We have no knowledge of the internal states of others, but we are aware of our corrupted and disturbed selves. Accordingly, give attention to your own internal condition. By focusing inward we will pursue self-correction instead of needlessly interfering in the affairs of others. We are not responsible for whether others wish to correct themselves or not.

If one holds a social position that requires him to be involved in the affairs of others, it is a difficult task.

---

131. Ayatullah Bahjat has said, "If you have negative assumptions towards your own worst enemy, which is your nafs, then you will have only positive assumptions about others and give them the benefit of the doubt." Available at https://bahjat.ir/fa/content/10863.

But, it should still not be that the deficiencies of the public bathroom are more important to us than the deficiencies of our own living room. We should be apprehensive about our own faults. We do not know if someone who we are finding fault with is a layperson or one of the *Awliya*. We do not correctly recognize laypeople, and the choicest servants of Allah (s) are even more hidden.

In a *Hadith al-Qudsi* Allah (s) said, "My *Awliya* are under my cloak."[132] In another narration it says, "My *Awliya* are under my cloak, and no one recognizes them but me."[133] Someone may pass by us without us recognizing them or their rank. Allah (s) has hidden his *Awliya* under his cloak, meaning others cannot access them easily. In truth, either their existence or their station is hidden from us. Many of the *Awliya* have come and gone, and no one recognized them at all. No one! And, even those whom people have recognized, they have done so to the extent that they say, "He is among the *Urafa*, the *Awliya*." The statement, "My *Awliya* are under my cloak," similarly holds true here. Have we recognized even one of the thousands of spiritual stations this individual traversed?

For example, that we know Allamah Tabataba'i was among the *Awliya* and *Urafa* does not mean we have recognized him.[134] Therefore, we may not recognize the

---

132. See Bahjat al-Taifeh, Ammar Badlisi, p. 54.
133. Ibid.
134. Ayatullah Muhidin Anwar said, "Ayatullah Shahabadi lived in Qom

Awliya of Allah (s), and if we recognize them by name, we still do not fully recognize their station. Generally, we must assume that whomever we encounter is one of the *Awliya*. Thereafter, we must be careful of our own actions and must not constantly find faults in others.

If we hold a negative opinion about others, we will always notice their faults. But, if we do not have a negative outlook in relation to others and if we are apprehensive about correcting ourselves, we will not have an opportunity to be occupied with the faults of others. As Imam Ali (a) has said in *Nahjul Balagha*, "Glad tidings to the one who has occupied himself with his own shortcomings such that he has no time for the shortcomings of the people."[135] The soul's faults are so numerous that they can occupy one forever. The soul is not like a material body, about which we can say after some time, "Now I have fixed my body, so I have time to find faults in others!"

When someone thinks his spiritual condition has been corrected, he actually possesses the greatest of spiritual defects. The faults of the soul have no end, so when man is careful about his own self, he is not occupied by the faults of others. Rather, he is engrossed in correcting himself. Perhaps others have a relationship with Allah (s) that we are not aware of. We do know, however, that our

---

in such a manner that most did not recognize his knowledge or spiritual station..." Insan-e-Kamil, p. 71.

135. See Footnote 101 and Nahjul Balagha, p. 255.

sins have ruined our connection with Allah (s), yet we are not concerned with correcting ourselves nor are we apprehensive about reconciling with Him. In truth, we want others to reconcile with Allah (s), but we do not pursue this reconciliation ourselves. The following is attributed to the poet Sharyar, "O Shahryar! Reconcile with God, although for reconciliation you have not left any place."

Enjoining Good and Forbidding Evil

Our spiritual teacher stated, "However, the obligation to enjoin good and forbid evil is another matter." If someone performs an evil act it does not make them a bad person, and we should not hold a bad opinion about them or speak about them behind their back. Rather, we should forbid the individual from performing the act. Discussing actions is different than discussing the individuals who perform those actions. If one performs a bad act or fails to perform a good act, we should enjoin good or forbid evil in relation to that act.

For example, someone performs a bad action in public, such as littering. One should advise them privately and with the utmost respect and etiquette that the place for garbage is not the ground and that it is not an appropriate action for a man of God. We should not, however, speak about this action behind the individual's back. Enjoining good and forbidding evil are indisputable matters, but a bad action does not make someone a bad person. Do not see the person as bad or hold a bad opinion about them. In truth, we should be sensitive toward the action, which is either good or bad, by enjoining good or forbidding evil, but we should not associate the action with the person's essence, as one's essence is separate from one's actions. However, those whose actions are public knowledge are not included in this calculation. For example, some say, "How do you know Yazid is wretched? We have no information about his heart." Such a statement about one who was a criminal throughout his life is laughable.

If we wish to look at others through a negative and pessimistic lens, it will appear that many are not among the people of guidance. But Allah (s) and his *Awliya* do not see the world as such. Imam Husayn (a) attracts those who have spent a lifetime sinning, and they elevate from the lowest to the highest of spiritual stations. This occurs because Imam Husayn (a) does not consider such individuals to be essentially bad. He (a) instead sees that they performed a bad action. Many who perform bad actions later obtain deliverance. We should sincerely pray for those who perform bad actions.

This etiquette is for all Muslims, but it is especially for those on the path of spiritual wayfaring. They should always suspect their own soul and ensure that they do not see anyone as being worse than them. Meaning, one should not consider oneself better than anyone, even one who drinks alcohol. After all, this is a bad action, but you are not in position to say, "This person is worse than me." If someone says my handwriting, painting, or carpentry skills are better than yours, there is no problem with such remarks if they are accurate. However, if one then takes such actions in aggregate and states, "I am better than you," this is problematic and incorrect.

When one says, "I am better than you," it means that

you are no good. It means we see you in a negative light and consider you to be insignificant, and this is inappropriate. It is possible for one to be better than another in a particular area. For example, one may be able to write, draw, drive, or derive Islamic law better than another person. But, none of these skills is the criterion by which we can judge if someone is actually better than another.

In summary, there are three points to keep in mind: first, everyone should see themselves and their actions through a negative lens and see others through a positive lens; second, enjoining good and forbidding evil are indisputable matters and do not impact our first duty of seeing others through a positive lens; and third, seeing others through a positive lens does not mean we give the worst of criminals a free pass and say, "Perhaps Yazid did not have bad intentions." We should not consider those whose evil actions are apparent to be good.

In relation to the worst of criminals, we would not have seen them as our enemies if they had not partaken in blatantly criminal actions. Just one of their actions, however, is enough for us to have enmity towards them for eternity. If Yazid and Shimr had not done what they did, we would not even recognize their names in the pages of history. That Allah (s) has dealt with them in a manner that their actions are seen as their essence is beyond us.

Finally, sometimes it is said that there are indicators

that so-and-so is working for the enemies of Islam and the Muslims, and that based on these indicators, one should exercise precaution. Generally, it is advisable that in places where oppressive governments rule, one should observe precaution about all people, except those one knows well.

Etiquette 13
Freeing the Soul

"All of one's struggles and difficulties are to strengthen the spirit so the soul frees itself from this natural world. Efforts must be made to strengthen the spirit, which lies in giving importance to the matters mentioned in this letter as much as possible, and in avoiding the strengthening of one's material aspects more than is necessary."

Prepare for the Journey

In truth, Etiquette 13 encompasses all of the prior 12 etiquettes, while simultaneously being an independent matter. On one hand, our spiritual teacher said to act on the 12 aforementioned etiquettes to strengthen the soul. At the same time, there are actions other than what has been mentioned here which must be performed to strengthen the soul.

Our spiritual teacher stated, "All of one's struggles and efforts are so the soul is strengthened." We have one body and one soul. Our body is made from clay, and it will return to clay. Our body is the mount and our soul is the rider. Our body is fashioned and our soul the fashioner. Our body is the servant and our soul the master. The body is a tool that the soul uses to reach its goals, Just like when one extends his hand to grab something.

The body can be used as a tool for every action, good or bad. Thus, what is important is the source or the rider, which is the soul. Keeping this in mind, the vehicle (meaning the body) should be given attention only to the appropriate degree. We should not give it as much importance as we give to the rider (the soul). The vehicle has importance, but its importance lies in it being a means for the rider to reach his destination. So long as the soul is in the body, it uses it to obtain its desires, elevate, and reach perfection. But when the soul and the body separate, the soul can no longer use the body, nor does it have any need for the body. It transfers to a world with different requirements.

Upon death, the body and the soul begin different journeys: the body goes beneath the soil, whereas the soul is transferred to another world and begins a new and eternal life which relies upon that which was obtained in this world. Thus, we know that the soul is important and must be strengthened, and that the body does not last forever. After death, our souls exist either within themselves or within a body, not like the one of this world, but rather a body appropriate for the requirements of the next world. In truth, that body which wishes to work in such difficult circumstances must be other than what we have now.

For example, if one wishes to work in an extremely hot environment, one must wear special clothing that can withstand high temperatures because his body cannot survive in that environment for even a minute. We will live in an immaterial world, and what is required there is this soul along with a body suitable for that world. Our bodies are connected to us until the moment we die, and in the next world these bodies have no role. Accordingly, we should give only the appropriate amount of importance to our bodies, knowing we will live only 50, 80, or 100 years. On the other hand, we should give importance to our souls in accordance with their eternal existence!

Constantly being preoccupied with matters related to the management of our bodies, such as our food, clothing, homes, or positions, causes us to become negligent of matters related to the soul. In truth, we misuse our souls when we employ them to serve our bodies. Saadi once said, "My precious life was spent in considering what I am to eat in the summer and wear in the winter."[136] What kind of life is that? This lifespan was gifted to us so our souls could prepare for eternity, but instead we waste it by focusing on this very world.[137] Therefore, give attention to the fact that this body is only worth its own usage, which is that of a vehicle.

Our spiritual teacher said that all of our struggles and efforts are so the soul is strengthened, as this soul is meant to last forever. Whatever action one performs, good or bad, they will see it. "Whoever acts righteously, it is for his own soul…and whoever does evil, it is to its detriment…"[138] From another perspective, Allah (s) states, "So whoever does an atom's weight of good will see it."[139] This means it is not as though one performs no good actions here and then when he reaches the hereafter everything will be prepared for him

---

136. Gulistan of Saadi, hikayeh 36.
137. Ayatullah Sa'adat Parwar said, "Appreciate the importance and opportunity of being young! Very few appreciate this blessing or spend this time working on themselves and correcting their deviations." Pand Nameh-e-Sa'adat, Sa'adat Parwar, p. 40.
138. Holy Qur'an, 41:46 - مَّنْ عَمِلَ صَالِحًا فَلِنَفْسِهِ وَمَنْ أَسَاءَ فَعَلَيْهَا وَمَا رَبُّكَ بِظَلَّامٍ لِّلْعَبِيدِ
139. Holy Qur'an, 99:7 - فَمَنْ يَعْمَلْ مِثْقَالَ ذَرَّةٍ خَيْرًا يَرَهُ

in the best manner. Rather, the good actions performed here take on a metaphysical reality there, and one sees the reality of that very action performed in this world, be it a heavenly or hellish reality. Therefore, strengthening the soul here—by recognizing Allah (s) and performing good deeds—beautifies and corrects the soul such that it benefits one in the hereafter. Accordingly, our teacher said that to strengthen the soul one must act on the 12 aforementioned etiquettes.

Death and Freedom

When man dies, the soul abandons this world, seperating from the body and continuing its journey while the body returns to dust. In truth, the Angel of Death, Azrael, helps us sinners by accelerating death.[140] Death enables the soul to become free from the body and to see its perfections, for so long as the soul is within the body it will not witness its true perfections. Azraeel is good, and we must respect him. In truth, he comes and rescues the soul from the body in which it has been imprisoned. The soul desires many things which the body lacks the capacity for, or which the body does not permit. When the soul obtains separation from the material world, it reaches its goal and its perfection. Thus, we must strengthen the soul to obtain this freedom.

This can be accomplished by adhering to the 12 aforementioned etiquettes, such as performing obligatory acts, avoiding prohibited acts, speaking an appropriate amount, not spending too much time with worldly people, not giving all of one's attention to one's food, not chasing after one's desires, pondering before taking any action, avoiding useless remarks, not holding frivolous gatherings,

---

140. It is related that Ayatullah Bahjat once said, "After death, every single person will wish they had died sooner. The people of heaven will wish they had died sooner to enjoy the heavenly blessings, and the people of hell will wish they had died sooner so they would not have accumulated so many sins." [Translator]

etc. If one acts on *The Etiquettes,* slowly one will separate and free oneself from this lowly world. This separation is in truth the strengthening of the soul. Meaning one is now prepared to traverse to another world where one can see, hear, and benefit from that which they obtained in this world by way of correct beliefs and righteous actions.

Act on *The Etiquettes* as Much as Possible

Our spiritual teacher also said "as much as possible," and this phrase has a profound meaning that is different from what we may assume. Allah (s) states in the Holy Qur'an, "Allah does not task any soul beyond its capacity."[141] For example, you want to lift weights. After lifting 10 pounds, do you then say, "This is the most I can lift"? No, rather you lift the heaviest amount possible to determine your capacity. This is what capacity means. It means that we go forward until we have exerted all our strength and reached our capacity, beyond which Allah (s) gives us no further duty. When our spiritual teacher says to give importance to the matters mentioned in this letter "as much as possible," we must take these matters seriously and truly advance as much as possible. It is not enough that when we do not easily reach our goals we say, "Refinement of the soul is beyond my capacity. I have no duty."

---

141. Holy Qur'an, 2:286 - لاَ يُكَلِّفُ اللَّهُ نَفْسًا إِلاَّ وُسْعَهَا

Preoccupation with Material Concerns

Finally, Ayatullah Sa'adat Parwar advised us to avoid strengthening the material aspects of our lives more than necessary. We spend much of our lives preoccupied with material concerns, such as the taste of our food, the color of our clothes, that our furniture matches our curtains, that we have the latest model car, etc. These matters are irrelevant, however, to our basic needs for food, rest, or transportation. Giving attention to such matters is an instance of being attached to this world and being held captive by one's lower desires. Put another way, it is the same problem as giving too much attention to the body. These are things we should avoid. On the Day of Judgment, we will not be questioned about the color or model of a particular item or whether our clothes did not perfectly match. Rather, we may be asked where we obtained our clothes or why we were so preoccupied with our bodies at the expense of our souls. We may be asked, "Did you think you would meet us with your physical body? Was it not the case that your soul was supposed to use your body to become stronger and worthy of meeting us? Where did you get lost? Why did you not minimize your preoccupation with the material world to only that which was necessary? Why did you not detach yourself from the world as much as possible?!"

At that moment we will have no answer. Thus, as much as possible, a wayfarer must keep aloof from materialism and only engage the material world to the extent necessary.¹⁴² For example, a car is a necessity, but giving unneeded attention to the model of the car is not. Now, there comes a time when one wishes to purchase a reliable car to get to work or school, and this is not a problem. What is a problem in this example is the obsession with the type of car one is purchasing and the hope that others will say, "Did you see the car so-and-so is driving?!" Recall that our Prophet (s) rode a donkey—do we really need a luxury car?

It is said that if someone has a home through which he wishes to attract people's attention, he is among the people of hell. The house which was meant to be a shelter from the cold and heat has become hellfire for him and will manifest as such in the next world. The house that was meant to fulfill legitimate needs, such as inviting friends over, holding a class, or other legitimate usages, has become hellfire.

It should be noted however, that the matter of what material items are appropriate for each person varies. Thus, for some a four-bedroom home is adequate and for someone else a two-bedroom home may be too large and for someone else an eight-bedroom home may be too small. What is important is that whatever we possess is necessary

---

142. Sayyid Ahmad Khomeini was once sitting on a worn-out rug at the home of Ayatullah Sayyid Ali Khamenei. He inquired about the rug and came to know it dated back nearly four decades, to the time of Ayatullah Khamenei's marriage. See Mutahhari, p. 141.

in relation to our legitimate needs.[143]

---

143. Imam Ali (a) said, "This world is a place for which destruction is ordained for its inhabitants and departure from here is destined. It is sweet and green, and it hastens towards its seeker and attaches to the heart of the viewer. So depart from here with the best of provisions available to you, and do not ask herein more than what is enough, and do not demand from it more than subsistence." Nahjul Balagha, Sermon 45.

Final Remarks[144]

Peace and blessings to my beloved brothers and sisters, wherever you may be. For those who have read this book and wish to reach the reality of existence, know this: The Creator of all creation is One! The God of all people is One! Whether we are black or white, from the East or from the West, Allah (s) sent the Holy Messenger Muhammad (s) for the guidance of all of humanity. Similarly, Allah's (s) commands in the Holy Qur'an are directed towards all of humanity.

Whatever our background, wherever we live, wherever we are from, Allah (s) invites us to spirituality when He says, "Soon we shall show them our signs in the horizons and in their own souls until it becomes clear to them that He is the Real…"[145] This shows us that the path to know Allah (s), to reach perfection, and to reach high spiritual stations, is open to all. Allah's (s) expectation is that we each pursue this path to our own capacity.

Take steps to know your Creator and travel this path. It is your destiny! Man is not confined to this world, even while living here. We must obtain the capacity to

---

144. Ustadh Vazirifard graciously provided the Final Remarks specifically for this translation. I express my sincerest gratitude to him for his constant support during the course of this project. [Translator]

145. Holy Qur'an 41:53 - سَنُرِيهِمْ ءَايَٰتِنَا فِى ٱلْءَافَاقِ وَفِىٓ أَنفُسِهِمْ حَتَّىٰ يَتَبَيَّنَ لَهُمْ أَنَّهُ ٱلْحَقُّ ۗ أَوَلَمْ يَكْفِ بِرَبِّكَ أَنَّهُ عَلَىٰ كُلِّ شَىْءٍ شَهِيدٌ

benefit from the higher realms of existence to someday benefit from the blessings that exist in eternal life. No one, no matter where you are from, or where you live, is less deserving of this blessing. All must struggle in this path and the path of spiritual wayfaring is open to all. I pray that whoever and wherever you are, you benefit from the spiritual reminders that Allah (s) gifts you and that you traverse this enlightened path.

What has been mentioned in this book were some matters which, according to our teacher Ayatullah Sa'adat Parwar, if acted upon would have a tremendous effect on one's spiritual growth and journey towards self-perfection and the meeting with Allah (s). Humbly, we ask Allah (s) to give us the tawfiq to act on these recommendations and etiquettes. I wish you every success. All praises are due to Allah (s), Lord of the worlds, and may the peace and blessings of Allah (s) be upon you.

Notes

Notes

**Oh Allah bless Muhammad and
the Family of Muhammad**

www.ingramcontent.com/pod-product-compliance
Lightning Source LLC
Chambersburg PA
CBHW050111170426
43198CB00014B/2532